FRANK SIDGWICK'S DIARY
AND OTHER MATERIAL RELATING TO
A. H. BULLEN AND THE
SHAKESPEARE HEAD
PRESS
AT STRATFORD-UPON-AVON

Julius Shaw's house in Stratford-upon-Avon

FRANK SIDGWICK'S DIARY

AND OTHER MATERIAL RELATING TO

A. H. BULLEN, & THE

SHAKESPEARE HEAD

PRESS

AT STRATFORD-UPON-AVON

OXFORD

PUBLISHED FOR THE

SHAKESPEARE HEAD PRESS

BY BASIL BLACKWELL

1975

INTRODUCTION

By ANN BAER, *daughter of Frank Sidgwick*

I WAS AWARE, for as long as I remember, that my father had worked at the Shakespeare Head Press in Stratford-upon-Avon some time early this century, but exactly when and in what circumstances I never really knew. It was not until my mother's death in 1973 (more than thirty years after my father's death) that this Diary was discovered. It was written in a small notebook which, having lost its spine, stood anonymously among hundreds of books in my mother's house. Also among my mother's possessions was found a large envelope on which my father had written "Shakespeare Head Press Oddments. Menu (signed) AHB Dinner". This is reproduced among the illustrations.

Mr Bullen, who, literally, dreamt up the S.H.P.* and at once followed up his dream with Biblical faith, was a scholar of Elizabethan literature and a publisher. I have two scraps of information about him – he breakfasted habitually on beer and steak, and bore so close a resemblance to Mark Twain, that when Mark Twain was reported to be in London, people pointed out Mr Bullen, whispering "that's Mark Twain". He took my father, who was recently down from Cambridge, into his publishing firm in 1901. Mr Bullen was also a friend of my *maternal* grandfather and my parents met through him.

The Diary records, in my father's small handwriting, the day to day events in starting the S.H.P. from 25 May 1904, to 23 March 1905, when he returned to London, and Mr Bullen arrived in Stratford to take it over. Mr Bullen continued the S.H.P. in Stratford until his death in 1920 when Basil Blackwell formed a small company to acquire it.

My father illustrated the Diary with photographs of the

---

* *Throughout its existence, both under Bullen's management and that of Sir Basil Blackwell, the Press was known as S.H.P. to everybody associated with it.*

interior and exterior of the house, which he stuck in to the notebook. A few notes in red ink, mostly explanations of technical terms, were added by my father, I presume at a later date. These, with a few pencil notes I have added myself, mostly to give the full names of people mentioned only by initials, are printed as footnotes.

The original Diary is now kept with other S.H.P. mementoes at Blackwells.

In reading the Diary I cannot but be impressed with the varied abilities that my father, who was then 24 or 25, displayed in starting a printing works in a small private house in a country market town all from scratch. He was machine-buyer, typesetter, gardener, book-keeper, personnel officer, typographer, paper-buyer, wages clerk, proof-reader, he devised the printers' work sheets, he set and printed the letter-heading on his little hand press, he composed and printed the menus for the Christmas dinner, he designed showcases and drying racks, he bought furniture, he addressed and filled envelopes. One may wonder *why* he kept the Diary at all, but anyone who knew him well would not find it strange. Meticulous recording of events was a pleasure to him.

I cannot help comparing the venture of S.H.P. as it was in 1904 with somewhat similar ventures in publishing in my own life. In 1904 it seems that technical help came, and promptly, simply for the asking (did Mr Jacobi of Chiswick Press do all he did just for the love of printing?). One cannot help noticing the speed with which repairs were done, supplies received, letters answered and proofs read.

There is one story which I remember overhearing my father telling which must have happened while he was in Stratford, but which he probably thought too insignificant to be recorded in the Diary. One day a Stratford working-class woman came to the S.H.P. saying she had heard that the young gentleman was interested in old books. She had an old book that had been knocking around her house for as long as she, and her mother, could remember. It had no cover on it, so she did not know what it was, sometimes the children had scribbled on it and sometimes had torn pages out, but when she pulled it from her shopping bag there was enough left for my father to identify a Second Folio Shakespeare. "I gave it back to her of course," he said, "in that state it had absolutely no value, but it was interesting to think that probably Shakespeare already had sufficient reputation in his hometown for a Second Folio to have found its way there and somehow, unrecognised to have survived, perhaps among the descendants of the owner's servants."

I sent the Diary to Sir Basil Blackwell who read it eagerly and proposed that it should be printed with supporting documents as a memorial of the founders of the Shakespeare Head Press. I am grateful for his interest and for the skill and care which Mr Ruari McLean has devoted to the production of the book.

In Sir Basil's enthusiasm I recognise the same mixture of pleasures that I share, and, as is so apparent from the Diary, that my father also shared — the pleasures in the well-set page, in lovely paper, in binding, and in regarding *fun* as part of the end-product as well as something worth publishing and a pleasure to read.

CONTENTS

ILLUSTRATIONS

DRAMATIS PERSONAE

A. H. BULLEN, a publisher and editor
F. SIDGWICK, his partner, and author of this Diary—Odd-job man } Manager owners of the Press

C. T. JACOBI, managing-partner of the Chiswick Press, London. Adviser to the Press.

A. C. WYATT, artist. Original lessee of the premises of the Press. *Left Aug.* 31, 1904

MESSRS H. W. CASLON, of London, type-founders to the Press.

MESSRS JOHN ESSON AND SON, of London, printers' engineers to the Press.

SIDNEY LEE, Shakespearian expert and enthusiast. Friend to the Press.

H. G. WEBB, owner of the Caradoc Press, London. Adviser to the Press.

C. T. WHITE, press-reader of the Chiswick Press, press-reader to the Press.

MESSRS SPICER BROS LTD, of London and Alton, Hants, paper-makers to the Press.

J. BLOMFIELD, of the Chiswick Press and Caradoc Press, technical instructor to the Press. Temp.

M. COOK, printer's foreman to the Press. *Left Nov.* 12, 1904.

F. COOPER, machinist to the Press.

F. SCOTT, compositor to the Press. *Left Sept.* 3, 1904.

J. H. PICKWORTH, compositor to the Press.

W. H. WESSON, compositor to the Press.

D. MEE, gardener to the Press. *Left Sept.* 29, 1904.

W. J. REDDING, boy-factotum to the Press.

ALBERT BRIDGER, office-boy to the Press.

H. PICKWORTH, boy at bindery.

T. SUMMERTON, printer's foreman, successor to Cook.

A. PALMER, bindery-foreman.

MISS WEBB, bindery-forewoman.

MISS PITCHER, folder and collator. *Left Feb.* 11, 1905.

DIARY

of the

SHAKESPEARE HEAD PRESS

STRATFORD-ON-AVON

adorn'd with elegant sculptures

PRELIMINARY

TOWARDS the end of the summer of 1903, A. H. Bullen, publisher, of 47 Great Russell Street, London, dreamt that he was on a visit to Stratford-on-Avon, and that just as he was leaving, someone approached him, saying "You must have a copy of this before you go: look, SHAKES-PEARE'S Works, printed here, by his fellow-townsmen!" A.H.B. remembers thinking in his dream, "By Jove, that is a good idea: I must remember that *when I wake.*" (The S.P.R.* should note this.) The following morning, he revealed the scheme to me, as his partner; and we continued for some time making estimates, and getting other information, both visiting Stratford for different purposes.

During the autumn and winter of 1903–4, several indivi-

* *The Society of Psychical Research.*

duals and firms were approached on the chance of their being willing to finance the scheme. Mr C. T. Jacobi (*managing partner of the Chiswick Press,*), unable to do so, nevertheless keenly interested himself and gave advice and assistance. Mr H. G. Webb (*owner of the Caradoc Press*) also gave practical advice. Edgar Morris Esq, Percy Spalding Esq (of Messrs Chatto and Windus) and Messrs William Clowes and Son, were approached without success. Mr Frank Pacy of the Kensington Public Library, and Mr G. W. Eccles of the Library Agency, were also admitted to the secret. (*Afterwards Mr Sidney Lee and others, before the final announcement.*)

On May 9, 1904, A.H.B. and F.S. visited Stratford, and interviewed A. C. Wyatt Esq, artist, then in occupation of 21 Chapel Street, formerly the house of Julius Shaw, one of the witnesses of Shakespeare's will: Mr Wyatt agreed to sublet part of the premises with a probable occupation of the whole afterwards.

Definite estimates were then obtained for type, machine and other plant, and orders given.

1904

MAY 25 WEDNESDAY. Left town by the 4.00 train G.C.R.*
arriving here at Stratford-on-Avon at half-past six, and put
up at the Red Horse. Saw Mr A. C. Wyatt at 21 Chapel
Street, and inspected our new premises, with a view to
calculating whether the machine can be got in.

MAY 26 THURSDAY. Carried various paraphernalia up to
Chapel Street, and went on to the East and West Junction
station. Goods from Esson's† arrived but no machine. Told
them to deliver at Chapel Street about 2, when the engineer
from Esson's arrived. Went to G.W.R.‡ station to look for
machine, but was told there is no goods delivery there.
Inquired for lodgings: am trying these at 22 Payton Street
until Saturday. Bought various stationery, and brought bag,
etc., round from hotel to lodgings. Met 12.35 at E&W.J.
station, Esson's engineer arriving thereby. Saw plant in
Goods Office with him, and learnt that machine was
probably at other (G.W.R.) station, the Goods station being
separate from the Passenger. On our way there, met the
machine and two cases. Adjourned for lunch. At 2.15 to
Chapel Street, and began carrying to first floor the plant,
which had already been delivered. Great tussle with the
imposing-surface. No sooner finished than machine arrived.
After more than two hours' labour we got it through the
front door into the entrance hall, where we left it for the
time being. Loose parts of machinery in two large cases:
opened these in street and carried them in singulatim – some
very heavy. Paid off men, and engineer departed until
required again. A heavy job and a warm rainy afternoon;
but "so far, so good", is the sum of the situation. The rain
prevented a crowd from gathering to watch the moving of

* *Great Central Railway.*
† *Printers' Engineers.*
‡ *Great Western Railway.*

the machine, which only attracted a few small boys and an odd ἐπιτυχών or two: partly due to Early Closing.

MAY 27 FRIDAY. Fitting imposing-surface* stand and frame† together all morning, also opening parcels of various fittings and arranging. No tools for bolting either. Frame rather puzzling to a novice, but it looks all right. Heavy rain all afternoon and evening.

MAY 28 SATURDAY. Spent morning in composing room with type-cases‡ and pigeon-holes, type having arrived overnight. The type itself too heavy to carry upstairs en masse. (Type is 1140 lbs in eight boxes of about 140 lbs each.) Midday train brought A.H.B. and Mr Jacobi down. Lunched at the Shakespeare Hotel, then inspected 21 Chapel Street, receiving advice and instructions from C.T.J. After a cup of tea with Mr Wyatt, we three walked round the town to show C.T.J. the places of interest. He says there should be no difficulty with machine: counsels us not to hurry – to the disturbance of A.H.B., who naturally wishes to see some tangible result as soon as possible. Also suggested a list of further desiderata. *Am to remain here through next week.*

MAY 30 MONDAY. Spent morning in repacking type-cases for return to Caslon's, to be exchanged for old-lay§ cases. Also packed rollers to go to Esson's to be covered with composition. Opened one box of type, and carried it up to the composing room piecemeal before lunch, and gave

---

* *The imposing-surface is a mathematically-flat-topped iron table, on which the composed type is placed, that it may present a level surface.*

† *The frames are the wooden stands which hold the type-cases for the compositor to work from.*

‡ *The type-cases are shallow boxes partitioned off into many small compartments to hold the types.*

§ *The "lay" of a case is the relative size and position of the various compartments. Messrs Caslon have invented a new lay, in which the various letters and spaces are so placed that composition is facilitated: but country printers being accustomed to the old lay, it was thought advisable to exchange.*

instructions for whitewashing the coal-house, which is to be used for the machine room. In the afternoon finished carrying the type upstairs – 1140 lbs in all. Carriers called for type-cases and rollers.

MAY 31 TUESDAY. Workmen in all day, whitewashing the machine room. The ink arrived – 4 lbs in four one-pound cans. Also presents from Caslon's representative, an old type-mould, and a small fount of black letter for me. Little to be done: made another attempt to put the stand of the imposing-surface together, or rather to put the bolts in: but the thread does not fit the sockets in all of them, and will have to be cut.

JUNE 1 WEDNESDAY. The extra frames, etc. arrived; and spent morning fitting together. Afternoon: cases arrived from Caslon's – old-lay exchanged for new-lay returned. Began laying* the type, and laid most of the lower case alphabet in the 14 pt size.†

JUNE 2 THURSDAY. Continued laying type all morning and afternoon, upper case and points and odd sorts; but did not touch the italics or the 11 pt fount. At about 3.30, the future overseer, one Cook, arrived, having been interviewed by A.H.B. yesterday. Apparently an able and experienced printer in all departments, about fifty or fifty-five, and rather slow in movement and speech: seems likely to be the very man we want. Inspected plant and arrangements, and considered the advisability of getting the machine in place tomorrow.

JUNE 3 FRIDAY. Again laying type, 14 pt italics in two double cases. Meanwhile Cook and two stalwart men (afterwards three) moved the machine from the front passage to

* *i.e. putting the various sorts of type in their respective compartments in the cases.*

† *We use two sizes: 14 pt or "English" size for the text, and 11 pt or "Small Pica" for songs (and stage-directions, afterwards altered). The lower case contains the small alphabet, points, and spaces; the upper case, capital letters and figures, etc.*

the machine room, somewhat damaging the glass-frame door, and removing a couple of bricks from the door-way of the machine room. However, it is cheap at the price, and things become shipshape rapidly.

JUNE 4 SATURDAY. Imposing-surface table bolted up and top put on. Laying of type still continues: numerous odd sorts and little room for them in the cases. Last two days magnificent weather.

JUNE 6 MONDAY. Finished laying type and putting away odd sorts. Cook began composing 4 pp. of *Tempest* by way of working specimen pages. I looked out for cheap furniture — table and chair for office-work: none to be found straight away. Knocked up a rough table out of type-boxes, in one of the attics, merely as a temporary convenience. Weather still glorious.

JUNE 7 TUESDAY. Composition continued. I began the preliminary matter to vol. 1, going to the Memorial Library to see the arrangement of the Dedication to the Earls of Pembroke and Montgomery. The 14 pt type turns out to be slightly larger than the English, so that the 38 lines of the specimen page (including the pagination at the foot) are equivalent to 37 of our 14 pt. But it appears to work out pretty level* in amount with the Dyce copy. The small pica (11 pt) will thus give a page of 59 or 60 lines solid. Proof and making-up papers ordered and planer† returned as faulty for exchange.

JUNE 8 WEDNESDAY. Prospectus copy to hand from A.H.B. Composed it myself all day, making just over a page set solid, but will doubtless look better when leaded out. A.H.B. has interviewed Sidney Lee, and interested him in the Press.

---

* *The proportions are about 8 pp. of our type to 7 of the Dyce edition, which we print from.*

† *The planer is a wooden brick used for beating the face of the type as it stands after composition on the imposing-surface.*

18

4 pp. of specimen matter put in chase by Cook, and 8 pp. altogether in type.

JUNE 9 THURSDAY. Composition continued. Rollers returned covered with composition from Esson. No news of the engine as yet, in spite of enquiries at the station.

JUNE 10 FRIDAY. Engine dispatched yesterday, but no advice received of it yet. A man of the name of F. Scott, a native of Stratford, called on me in the morning, saying he had heard there was a press here from a friend of his at Stanley's, the local printer in this street. Appeared to be nervous. Act I of the *Tempest* now up in type, and some pp. of preliminary matter in the small pica.

JUNE 11 SATURDAY. Engine still not to be seen. Composition continued. Act II of *Tempest* in progress. Return to town.

JUNE 13 MONDAY. To Stratford again, bringing my own little press. Fit it together: it will be useful for odd jobs, such as heading note-paper, to which I turn it at once.

JUNE 14 TUESDAY. Engine has been at station ever since Saturday, but could not be delivered without orders. Wired to Esson for these and engineer. Printed some note-paper heading. My composition of the prelim. delayed by lack of quads,* as most of it is commendatory verses.

JUNE 15 WEDNESDAY. Bought furniture (table 7/6, chair 3/6) nice old bits. Cook pulled two rough proofs of the first forme with the aid of my roller and the planer. Esson's engineer arrived, and arranged for delivery of gas-engine. It appears there may be trouble with the supply, and he recommends a separate meter.†

JUNE 16 THURSDAY. The machine and engine in course of erection all day. A.H.B. down for half-day and saw proofs;

* *Quads or quadrats are solid pieces of lead for filling spaces in the type, corresponding to white paper when printed.*
† *Which we had put in: also a separate connection with the gas-main. See June 18.*

19

rather doubtful as to size of two types, but will consult Jacobi. F. Scott (see June 10) taken on as compositor for a week's trial from tomorrow morning. Probably to be retained even if incompetent, to lend local colour to the scheme.

JUNE 17 FRIDAY. The machine completed: it is now possible to pull proofs by turning the fly-wheel by hand. First instalment of vellum to hand. New compositor Scott at work all day: Cook and engineer busy over engine and machine. Extra chases all too large and require filing down.

JUNE 18 SATURDAY. Gas company in, putting new connection and meter for gas-engine. Engine cemented down in its bed.

JUNE 20 MONDAY. Composition continues, though delayed by uncertainty. The small pica is condemned by Mr Jacobi for stage-directions, and the English will probably be substituted. Other alterations are also suggested as to enumeration of lines, head-lines, etc.

JUNE 21 TUESDAY. Engine finished and ran for a short while. Exhaust pipe requires staying as it vibrates a little. Finished setting Jonson's address in First Folio. Began on garden, which is in a terrible condition, but could not do much with a two-shilling spade. The engine belt arrived and was put on; the machine room is now in running-order, and at 5 o'clock the engine was turned on and belted to the machine and both ran together, the speed with slow gear working out to 1140 per hour. With rollers and impression, the extra resistance will doubtless reduce this to about 1000 impressions per hour. Cook and I were both instructed as to starting and stopping the engine. Engineer left.

JUNE 22–28 I was away, and A.H.B. was here. Pp. 1–32 were in chase, after alteration, and proofs pulled, which A.H.B. took away to read. Carpentry done – various odd jobs.

20

JUNE 29 WEDNESDAY. Composition and substitution (of 14 pt for 11 pt in stage-directions) continued. The exhaust of the engine was turned down into a bricked chamber in the ground, which is filled with coke and covered with a stone. This almost entirely silences the puff of the exhaust.

JUNE 30 THURSDAY. Attempted a title-page, but types too small at 18 pt, the largest we possess. *The Tempest* finished today: 70 pp. of our type weighing just over 7 lbs each. But we have now used all the 14 pt quads sent, though only about half the type is set up. Further supply ordered.

JULY 1 FRIDAY. Composed L. Digges' address and Dram. Pers. of *Two Gentlemen*. Bought Ledger and started the book-keeping. Proofs of first two sheets returned from A.H.B.

JULY 2 SATURDAY. Book-keeping morning. Caslon cannot cast figures as we wanted – 10 pt on 14 pt body – for numbering lines. Write to Jacobi about it. Gardening afternoon and evening.

JULY 4 MONDAY. Composition. New supply of 14 pt quads arrives. Also first instalment of paper – $4\frac{1}{2}$ reams.

JULY 5 TUESDAY. Second proofs of first 4 sheets pulled on the stone. Jacobi's reply about figures is to re-order them, saying Caslons have no right to hesitate.

JULY 6 WEDNESDAY. Proofs morning. Sidney Lee calls. Over birth-place with him and garden: Professor Van Dyke of Princeton. To Shottery with S.L.: over Anne Hathaway's cottage. Over these premises. One chase sent to Esson to measure new ones by.

JULY 7 THURSDAY. Caslon still make difficulties over the figures. A.H.B. arrives and will see Caslon's man in Jacobi's presence tomorrow. Read proofs with him, deciding minor points of style. Pull a proof or two on our paper, machine-bed made up by outside help.

JULY 8 FRIDAY. Crank-handle fitted to fly-wheel of machine, to pull proofs with, independently of the gas-engine, which refuses to act properly, and must be seen to. 3rd proofs pulled of first four sheets. Extra chases arrive.

JULY 9 SATURDAY. Proof-reading all morning. Question of figures at last arranged: Caslon's are to cut matrices of 10 pt figures on 14 pt bodies, and deliver as quickly as possible. Composition continued. Order sent for 40 lbs or so of odd sorts to level up 14 pt fount. New matter put in chase.

JULY 11 MONDAY. Show A.H.S.* over works. Proof-reading. Sheets F–I first proofs pulled. Read them all afternoon. Write C.T.J. about press-man.

JULY 12 TUESDAY. Proofs finished. Return for revise. Composition delayed: nearly all type is set, and locked-up waiting to be worked off.

> [*Meeting of Stratford Town Council, July* 12, 1904. – It was decided to offer Mr. A. H. Bullen a repairing lease of 21, Chapel-street, for fourteen years at £30 per annum, determinable by the lessee at the end of the seventh year. *Stratford-upon-Avon Herald, July* 15, 1904]

JULY 13 WEDNESDAY. Arrival of new sorts to level up fount. Formes corrected and proofs of F–I pulled, read, and sent to A.H.B. with revises of B–E. A.H.B. is advertising for a press-man. Mr Wyatt, who is looking out for another house – he has visited the Old Court House at Long Crendon, near Thame, Bucks – has applied for us to the Corporation regarding a long lease of this house, 21 Chapel Street. They reply they are willing to give a 14-year lease renewable after 7 years. A.H.B. asked for 21 years, renewable after and 7 and 14 years, but the other is quite sufficient.

JULY 14 THURSDAY. A.H.B. writes that he has nearly a score of replies to advt for a press-man, and expects more. He will then confer with Jacobi. (This should be entered

* *Arthur Hugh Sidgwick, the writer's brother.*

22

under tomorrow's date.) The need of beginning to print is pressing, as we have over 100 pp. composed, of which 64 are formes in 16 chases – all we have. Doubtless the simplest plan would be more chases, eight of which cost £3. Again, of the smaller-size type (11 pt), we have used all on the 16 pp. of prelims, and the songs in the *Tempest*. The prelim. is not in chase yet, and therefore it is so much type lying fallow, which we want for songs, etc. in the new matter. Luckily the *Two Gentlemen* and the *Merry Wives* do not contain many songs. Or perhaps *un*-luckily, from any but the typographical point of view.

JULY 15 FRIDAY. Occupied in composing and printing on my model press a Weekly Report or work-sheet. The little press is useful for small jobs of this kind. Also the *Shotover Sonnets* of C.S.S.* – rather an amateur result.

JULY 16 SATURDAY. Set up a slip for the machine room, to check no. of sheets of paper given out, perfected, and spoiled, and reason of spoilage.

JULY 18 MONDAY. Composition getting more difficult as we are in daily need of a press-man. At present we can only get the matter as nearly correct as possible without proofs. A.H.B. left the replies to the advt with Jacobi on Saturday, and is to consult him today.

JULY 19 TUESDAY. Letter from Esson's: A.H.B. has ordered eight more chases, and they want one as before to measure by. Composition now practically impossible: figures being put in formes and margins re-adjusted to suit. The proper figures have not come yet.

JULY 20 WEDNESDAY. Same work continued.

JULY 21 THURSDAY. Second instalment of paper. Also the figures arrive at last. A.H.B. down for half the day. Figures inserted in first four sheets B–E, which A.H.B. took away for Jacobi to read. Double order of chases and furniture.

* *Charlotte Sophia Sidgwick, the writer's mother.*

JULY 22 FRIDAY. All composition stopped, Scott away. A.H.B. will interview press-man today, in town. Cook cleaning up and doing odd jobs.

JULY 23 SATURDAY. Furniture arrives. Pay small a/cs and balance books. Insurance agent called.

JULY 25 MONDAY. Interview prospective gardener – a Yorkshireman. Revises of F–I returned from A.H.B. Press-man (Cooper) to arrive next Saturday. Revises put in hand.

JULY 26 TUESDAY. Press-reader's proofs returned (B–E) from A.H.B. The press-reader is the Chiswick Press man, Charles T. White. A.H.B. has engaged him to read the 10 vols at 1/- per sheet of 8 pp.

Leave Stratford (for wedding) till Monday next (Bank Holiday).

A.H.B. here Thursday 28–Saturday 30th, when Cooper the press-man arrived.

AUGUST 2 TUESDAY. First proofs of K–Q returned from A.H.B. Read K, L, M, N, and send to revise. Third delivery of paper. Gas-engine running again to ease working. Prepare subscription-register of names and addresses of all customers.

The gardener interviewed July 25, one David Mee, started work on Saturday, and is going ahead nobly.

AUGUST 3 WEDNESDAY. A Chiswick Press machine-man arrived by the 12.35 to start our work, and give Cooper tips – Blomfield by name. The first thing he pointed out was that the composition on the rollers is too thick, as it overlaps the "lifts", or bearing-wheels at the ends of the roller, by about an eighth of an inch. Temporarily this can be remedied by underlaying the roller-bearings, but one set of rollers was packed off to Esson's to be set right. Blomfield appears to know his business thoroughly, including vellum-printing. Two finished sheets were pulled to show margins, and sent off to A.H.B. Sidney Lee called again. Measured the garden and made plans.

24

AUGUST 4 THURSDAY. Blomfield's next discovery is that the machine works a little too fast – 1440 impressions per hour whereas we want about 1000. This must be remedied by having a smaller pulley wheel on the gas-engine. Write to Esson's about this. A.H.B. wires that Jacobi suggests a slight alteration in the side-margins of the pulls we sent yesterday – which I had indeed anticipated. Talk with Cook about his various short-comings; he is rather idle and inclined to drink and gossip – a dodderer.

AUGUST 5 FRIDAY. Specimen pull returned from Jacobi; inner margins, as I guessed, to be slightly reduced. F and G sent for press. K to press-reader, who also has H and I. Order metal furniture to safeguard against dropping in case of warped wood. Esson's write that the rollers are too large, because they have swelled by being kept in a damp place.

AUGUST 6 SATURDAY. Esson's dispatch the rollers this morning. The engine-pulley is being removed to return to them, when they will forward a smaller one: it appears a 7-inch diam. pulley will be about the size needed.

AUGUST 8 MONDAY. New rollers to hand: Blomfield thinks that after all they were cast too large, as, if the increase had been caused by damp, they would have swelled irregularly.

AUGUST 9 TUESDAY. Metal furniture to hand. Pulley arrives and is fixed on engine. Sigs. H, I and K, returned for press. Copy for *Measure for Measure* from A.H.B. with some ingenious emendations of his: the play, however, remains inscrutable in places. WE BEGIN TO PRINT. Signature C is the first in the press.

AUGUST 10 WEDNESDAY. Signature C finished, and the twelve vellum copies printed with no waste, under my own eyes. Arrange with Blomfield that he is to stay till Saturday.

AUGUST 11 THURSDAY. Sigs. B and K on machine running under Cooper's guidance. Blomfield has written out a scheme of instructions and suggestions regarding machining, and wetting the paper and the vellum. He suggests a second imposing-surface for the machine room. Probably a slate surface would do. We still find a need of certain letters, and another order must go to Caslon.

AUGUST 12 FRIDAY. Sig. B finished by Cooper under Blomfield's surveyance. Distribution now practicable. Borough Surveyor called and made measurements. The gardener last week found a gold coin of 1700 in the garden, but disposed of it out of Stratford before I could see it or make an offer for it. He called it "half a spade-guinea".

AUGUST 13 SATURDAY. Blomfield left, pretty well drained of technical information; I talked to him most of the morning. He has been simply invaluable in giving us a good start, and has gone out of his province to give me hints as to the management in the matter of weekly work-sheets, or bills of labour from each man.

Things are now going ahead, and the cares of government begin to press. A.H.B. has in tow one Millard, of McClurg and Co. of Chicago, to whom he has opened the scheme.

AUGUST 15 MONDAY. Second instalment of vellum to hand. Engaged one Redding, a boy, to be of general use, for a *5/-* weekly pittance. Further sorts to hand. K finished. Engaged a boy, by name Redding (son of the temporary carpenter who worked here in the beginning), — alas, this is repetition.

AUGUST 16 TUESDAY. Sig. D on machine. Return sorts to Caslon: they have sent the wrong italic capital T: *T* instead of *T*. New imposing surface arrives for the machine room.

AUGUST 17 WEDNESDAY. Sig. D finished: E put on. Expecting a visit from Marie Corelli, who has heard of the Press: but she doesn't come. Pamphlet of two lectures on typography from Jacobi.

AUGUST 18 THURSDAY. Sig. E finished during the day. A.H.B. down, settling many things. Cooper is to have 30/- a

26

week and 3/- for cleaning in overtime. Cook is not satisfied with Scott, and suggests a local man, named Pickworth, who wrote to me the other day, applying for a place. He seems to be a competent workman, but I should be sorry to lose Scott. We also talked of the title-page, in which I shall make experiments; the prospectus; the system of work-sheets, weekly for each man; the registration necessary for the boy, as he is under 18, and employed near machinery; and proofs. Wyatt wants us to buy £35 worth of his pictures, before clearing out, which in that case he undertakes to do at once. In any case we are to pay him £20 when he does go. But it may be worth our while to do so.

AUGUST 19 FRIDAY. Proof-reading all morning. Interview Pickworth, but cannot engage him yet. He is a native of Stratford. Trouble with our paper: Spicer's seem to be careless, and put up spotted and dirty sheets in the good reams as well as in the retree. Write to A.H.B. about it. Print a weekly time-sheet.

AUGUST 20 SATURDAY. F on machine. A.H.B. returns P and Q for press. R and S sent out to him. The gardener (Mee) has found a brass* token of 1794, which he does not value and has given me.

AUGUST 22 MONDAY. Rain all day: remove stock to inner kitchen. Re-sketch title-page, about which I am pretty well determined now: we are to have a printer's device on it, which will help. I expect the type for it tomorrow, when I shall begin to experiment.

> [*Meeting of Stratford Town Council, August 22, 1904.* —
> The seal of the Council was also affixed to two gas deben-
> tures and twenty general district fund debentures, and to a
> lease to Mr. A. H. Bullen of the house next to New Place.
> — *Stratford-upon-Avon Herald, August 25, 1904*]

* *The coin is a copper farthing-token of 1794, with letters round it signifying "Brunswickensis et Lunenbergensis Dux, Sacri Romani Imperii Archi-Thesaurius et Elector. 1794".*

AUGUST 23 TUESDAY. The type has not arrived. Help distribution: packing printed sheets. G finished: H on machine.

The trouble with the title-page is as follows: The words "William Shakespeare" should go on one line. Now the difficulty is to get a type, congruous with the old-face type used in the book, and thin enough to compose those words in one line, and yet large enough to catch the eye well. I expect Caslon's 20-pt Titling in the Old Face will do this, though it may look rather small. The gardener is procuring turf for the lawn from Shottery.

AUGUST 24 WEDNESDAY. Still the title-type has not arrived. Re-organise the prospectus, which I set up months ago (June 8). Sig. H on machine.

The double occupation of this house is giving great trouble: we ought to have got the Wyatts out sooner. They continue to use certain rooms for which we stipulated; doors left open, or doors left shut and found open, are the *casus belli*; and today there is a rubbish-heap set on fire by accident under their week's washing. *Hinc illae lacrimae.*

AUGUST 25 THURSDAY. Type and cases arrive. Set up title-page during morning and have it pulled. Another intestine row: this time with the gardener, who complains of the children running over newly raked earth. A.H.B. down, bringing H. G. Webb. After lunch, A.H.B. arranged the final departure of the Wyatts for today week, but it cost £35 worth of his pictures, as well as the £20 previously promised. But I think it is worth paying for. Meanwhile Webb and I looked over the stock of paper and vellum, and he considers we have just cause of complaint against the paper-makers, Spicer Bros. He took away some spotted sheets which he himself took out of a good ream, and will confront Augustine Spicer with them.

A.H.B. wants to go faster, and put in another machine. Cooper thinks there is not room.

28

AUGUST 26 FRIDAY. Carefully sort vellum all the morning, turning out sheets that are to go back and be doctored. Distribution and proof-reading in afternoon. Weather fine again after three weeks' dull and chilly weather: the gardener begins laying the Shottery turf. Wrote to Pickworth (see Aug. 19) engaging him as compositor from Sept. 5.

AUGUST 27 SATURDAY. T returned from A.H.B. Wrote to Dr Ross (of the corner house of Church Street and Scholar's Lane) who has a studio to let, which may suit us as a warehouse and bindery. Had to give Scott notice. He is a thoroughly energetic and willing workman, but too slow for us and unaccustomed to high-class bookwork.

AUGUST 29 MONDAY. Wyatts' moving preparations going ahead rapidly. Dr Ross wrote on Saturday that the studio was let to a music-teacher. Sheet L finished: Cooper anxious I should look it through before packing it away, to shift responsibility from his shoulders. *Re* another machine, he thinks there would be room for a "Colt" side by side with the "Mitre", driven from a pulley on the outside of the fly-wheel, as "Colt" machines drive from the left. In that case I should propose to substitute another window for the present door of the machine-room, and open the bricked-up door into the paper warehouse.

AUGUST 30 TUESDAY. Distribution. The house in confusion. Proofs, book-keeping, odds and ends. Sig. X out to A.H.B. M on machine. In the vellum of L one sheet slurred a little, and was reprinted. This is the first sheet of vellum we have spoiled in 10 signatures or 120 sheets or 240 printings.

AUGUST 31 WEDNESDAY. Departure of the Wyatts. Move my office from an awkwardly accessible attic to the room next to the composing room. Proofs. Sheet M finished. Inspect and turn out a few.

SEPTEMBER 1 THURSDAY. Print order form, and head five quires of note-paper with address. Sheet N finished, O on machine. Boy ill, and sent home. House comparatively quiet now the Wyatts are gone.

SEPTEMBER 2 FRIDAY. Proofs, Z revised, and AA 1st proof. Packing sorts in composing room. The charwoman cleans the house. Sig. O outer on machine: a narrow escape of printing the whole sheet minus a word (the word "forth", *The Two Gentlemen of Verona*, II, 4, p. 97, line 183) which Cooper found dropped almost as soon as he began. It was all right in the 1st press-pull,* but in the 2nd and colour-sheet I – alas! – failed to notice its omission. However, we are saved: though it indicates the care needed. Today it strikes me – as the result of a chase cracking at one corner – that it might be a good notion to make the kitchen into our composing room. This would do away with the carrying of the chases – 40 lbs-odd when full – up and down stairs: it would be more convenient for the machine room: it is quite as light and as large a room.

SEPTEMBER 3 SATURDAY. O finished: P on machine. Sigs. Z and AA sent out to A.H.B. Write to Caseley, the "professor of music" in possession of the studio (see Aug. 29) that we want for a bindery. Scott leaves.

SEPTEMBER 5 MONDAY. A.H.B. arrives midday. Chief discussion *re* counting, inspecting, and drying printed sheets. Decide to advertise for a bindery room or warehouse, and to get a drying-rack made.

SEPTEMBER 6 TUESDAY. Hang the vellum first three sheets to dry on strings in one of the attics. Design a drying rack for carpenter to estimate for. Draft advt for binding-warehouse. Sig. P finished: Q put on. First proofs of prelim.

** After the "press-proof" is returned, marked "press", the formes are put aside till needed for printing. When they are put on the machine, a "press-pull" is taken to see that each is correct. When finally passed, a pull on the proper paper is shown, in order to be sure that it is of the correct blackness – neither too much nor too little ink. This is called the "colour-sheet".*

30

SEPTEMBER 7 WEDNESDAY. Sidney Lee called: the people next door, the Savage family, who are mostly consumptive, are annoyed, it appears, with the noise made by the machine. One daughter in particular complains. But what can we do?

Interview carpenter *re* drying rack. A.H.B. returns X and Y for press.

SEPTEMBER 8 THURSDAY. R on machine. Distribution, and re-arrangement of cases. Alter sheets of vellum drying: B, C, D, dry: hang up E, F, G.

SEPTEMBER 9 FRIDAY. Our advt appears in the *Herald* for a workshop

> [WANTED to rent a WORKSHOP, or one or two Rooms suitable for Warehousing, &c. Must be dry, clean, well-lighted easy of access, and centrally situated. Write Julius Shaw, *Herald* Office.]

Simultaneously a second advt appears.

> [WEST STREET. – Commodious, well-lighted SCHOOL-ROOM to Let; perfect sanitary arrangements; possession at once. – Apply 6, Chestnut-walk.]

Went to inspect. The schoolroom would do admirably for our purpose: rent £10 per annum. Gas and water laid on: fireplace: skylights. Unluckily another man has first refusal. R finished, S put on.

SEPTEMBER 10 SATURDAY. Lay out 3 more sheets of vellum in front bedroom. Inspect sheet R. Interview Bailey the furniture-dealer; show him the house: he is to select bits for our approval. Sorts arrive from Caslon. Wages and weekly balancing of accounts.

SEPTEMBER 12 MONDAY. Letters both from Caseley the music-professor (see Sept. 3), saying he has no intention of giving up his studio; and from Mr, Mrs, or Miss Peart Bolland, of 6 Chestnut Walk, saying that the schoolroom is taken (see Sept. 9). So both strings to our bow snap together. Sheet S inspected: X put on. 1st proof of DD and revises of BB and CC.

SEPTEMBER 13 TUESDAY. Sheet X finished. Change vellum drying sheets in both rooms. Distribution. Sheet X is a little out of the proper register, and contains a broken em-rule. Sheets BB and CC sent out, DD for revise, A and *b* (prelim.) also sent out. T put on machine.

SEPTEMBER 14 WEDNESDAY. Proofs and dis. in the morning. Great trouble in the afternoon with the outer forme of T, the register of which is out.

SEPTEMBER 15 THURSDAY. A.H.B. down with Mr Blackwell, connoisseur of pictures, furniture, etc. to inspect Bailey's furniture and our house. Five pieces – a gate-legged table at £3.10, a sideboard £3.10, a settle £6.6.0, a Welsh cabinet £6, a nest of drawers on stand £4.4.0. – selected; Mr Bailey away in spite of arrangements made. Prospect for house for our bindery; it is hard to find a suitable place. U put on machine.

SEPTEMBER 16 FRIDAY. Bailey's estimate for the five pieces of furniture wired to A.H.B. – £23. He wires "Purchase". Still searching for a bindery. Trouble again with rollers. Inspect and count sheet T. 1026 good, seven or eight passable, and waste. Turn vellums drying.

SEPTEMBER 17 SATURDAY. Press-proofs of Y, Z, and AA. Interview Mr Deer, of Hutchings and Deer, regarding premises for bindery. BB and CC returned from A.H.B. Rollers and chases both giving trouble. Wages and accounts.

SEPTEMBER 19 MONDAY. Blocks of printer's device arrive, two of three ins. long and three of one-and-a-half. The fountain in the garden finished as far as may be before quite deciding what is it to be like. Inspect and count sheet U; 1025 good and passable, except that there is a "pick" off the roller on p. 152, Sc. III, line 8, word "I" in about 100 or 150 out of the thousand. It is very slight. Y put on machine after some trouble. Inspect the house next but one to Marie Corelli's and her property.

SEPTEMBER 20 TUESDAY. Vellums now dry as far as printed. Y finished, Z put on with no difficulties. Trellis being put up in garden. The large front room now has five fine old pieces of oak in it and several chairs.

SEPTEMBER 21 WEDNESDAY. Arrange about having gas put in the various rooms, for the winter. The men, Cook, Cooper, and Pickworth, want Saturday next till Monday noon off, to go to London on a jaunt, making up the lost time in overtime. This will suit very well, as the gas can be put in while they are away, and on the intervening Sunday I propose to transfer the composing room to the present kitchen.

Interview Marie Corelli's butler, Mr Bridger, about the semi-detached house next to hers. He says the rent is £40 on a half-yearly tenancy.

Inspect sheet Y. About half this sheet has a small 'pick' off the bad rollers, in the first half of the "w" of "way" on p. 168, line 73. I am keeping the formes back, and sending a sheet up to A.H.B. for him to decide whether we pass it, or reprint. All the vellums have the pick as well.

Another instalment of paper arrives, 39 ($20\frac{1}{2}/21\frac{1}{2}$) reams, all good. This we stock in the larder next to the kitchen, which will shortly be the composing room. – Mr Meadows, owner of No. 13, West Street, a house I have had my eye on for the bindery, calls: he is unwilling to let except as a permanency.

SEPTEMBER 22 THURSDAY. Prospectus made up for preliminary consideration. I composed it on June 8. Proofs pulled and one sent to A.H.B. Sheet Z inspected. Sheet AA finished, but with some nasty "picks" from the faulty rollers. 160 of them have a "space-up", which was my fault, and I shall have to scratch it out 160 times with penknife and eraser. DD and EE returned for press.

SEPTEMBER 23 FRIDAY. GG and HH sent out. Move my office from the small room next composing room to the front sitting room on first floor, making a larger table out of two small ones and planks. BB put on machine.

SEPTEMBER 24 SATURDAY. The men away. Gas-fitters in. With the boy's aid, transfer composing room downstairs to the kitchen, unbolting the frames and imposing-surface table, carrying them down piecemeal, and refitting: because the stair-way is too narrow to allow them being carried down bodily.

FF returned for press.

Gas-fitters working all afternoon.

SEPTEMBER 26 MONDAY. Gas-fitters in possession. Work-men return from London by the 12.35, which also brings A.H.B. and Miss Dorothea Bullen. House inspected. Gas-engine and machine not working all day, as gas-fitters still here. Visit Bailey and buy more furniture. Inspect Marie Corelli's semi-detached.

SEPTEMBER 27 TUESDAY. Scratch the "space-up" out of 100 sheets of AA. Interview Marie Corelli's companion or keeper, a Miss Byber (?) (*Vyver*) concerning the semi-detached. The Great Lady herself comes in. Very affable. Rent £42, to be taken for a year at least; no nameplate or signboard. Noise affects doctor next door rather than M.C.

SEPTEMBER 28 WEDNESDAY. New roller on machine. Write A.H.B. about M.C. house for bindery. Over to Leamington for sale of furniture at hotel. Buy nothing.

SEPTEMBER 29 THURSDAY. A day of troubles. First the rollers go again. Cooper suspects the fault lies in the drum of the machine. Write at length to Esson's about it. Second-ly, on p. 196, in the bottom line, two or three letters broke, half-way through printing, and the fault was not observed until I came to look at finished sheet. 600 paper and all vellums of CC are thus imperfect. Write to Marie Corelli to take house for bindery. In and out of Corn Exchange all day attending furniture sale. Buy an oak chest for 10/-. To top

34

all, a heavy cold in the head. The gardener has finished his work, and leaves.

SEPTEMBER 30 FRIDAY. DD on machine, II and KK first proofs. Interview Mr Bridger, Marie's butler (see Sept. 21) and his son Albert, with the idea of engaging the latter as reading-boy. I think he will suit, at 5/- a week, and is willing to make himself generally useful.

OCTOBER 1 SATURDAY. Note from Marie Corelli's companion Miss Vyver (see Sept. 27 misspelt) accepting our tenancy of No. 7 Church Street for one year at £42 with option of renewal and 3 months' notice. A.H.B. has seen Jacobi and Blomfield about Thursday's difficulties: they neither believe anything wrong with machine: and Jacobi says "pen-and-ink" for the 600 sheets with broken letters – nice little job for me. Up to town. See A.H.B. in the afternoon. He shows me some sample bindings – rather cheap and nasty. Must get something better.

OCTOBER 3 MONDAY. London. Call Chiswick Press. See Jacobi about things in general and Blomfield about the roller-question. To Stratford. The quire-stock is now removed to the bindery at 7 Church Street. Sig. EE on machine. New office-boy (see Sept. 30) Albert Bridger, in attendance afternoon.

OCTOBER 4 TUESDAY. EE finished. DD inspected. Make experiments as to supplying the missing letters in CC: pen-and-ink seems better than stamping in. FF put on.

OCTOBER 5 WEDNESDAY. A.H.B. returns M.C.'s agreement-to-let approved: send it back signed. EE inspected and counted. Tremendous labour over outer forme of FF; the whole morning wasted by Cook's lack of common-sense. Pickworth put on the job: he gets it right. M.C.'s counterpart agreement to hand: also key of 7 Church Street. Zaehnsdorf's and Douglas Cockerell's books on bookbinding arrive: I study them. More furniture from Bailey.

OCTOBER 6 THURSDAY. Arrange with carpenter to make shelving at bindery. HH and II returned for press: LL first proof: FF inspected.

OCTOBER 7 FRIDAY. GG on machine: open forme with change of play and blank page in it. Two chases returned with bars: GG put into these, and no difficulty of register at all.

OCTOBER 8 SATURDAY. HH put on: difficulties again, but not serious. MM first proof. C.S.S.* comes down: show her over. Wages and weekly accounts.

OCTOBER 10 MONDAY. Inspect GG: it is overprinted (1050). Carpet for front room due and expected, but does not arrive: clean up in anticipation. Bailey calls about other carpets and furniture. Revise of prospectus to hand. A.H.B. has at last allowed his name to appear as editor of the text. Blackwell has suggested to him the brilliant idea of dedicating the edition to the King. Pickworth suggests that as we have rooms to spare at 7 Church Street (hereinafter styled the bindery), he should live there with his sister. I think this might be an excellent plan. Write A.H.B. about it.

OCTOBER 11 TUESDAY. Inspect HH. Carpet arrives and put down. In expectation of photographer tomorrow, rooms are prepared for him to photograph. KK put on. Front room now complete.

OCTOBER 12 WEDNESDAY. The day of Stratford "Mop" Fair. Copy for booklet of the S.H.P. Letter of dedication to the King. Inspect II. Remove vellums drying and carry iron bed-stead on which they were drying upstairs, a tight fit. KK put on with trouble: the worst sheet yet.

OCTOBER 13 THURSDAY. KK finished. Revise of prelim. A – title-sheet: final revise, I hope. Cook is really intolerable, and we must get rid of him. Composing specimen p. of

* *Charlotte Sophia Sidgwick.*

36

booklet, in order to keep an eye on him in the comp. room. Sheet *b* of prelim. prepared for press.

OCTOBER 14 FRIDAY. New rollers to hand. Bailey calls about furniture. In comp. room most of morning. Inspect half of KK which is only fair, but will have to do. Inquire about a hand-cart for transference of stock. New rollers on machine, for the small pica in prelim. Prospectus returned for press.

OCTOBER 15 SATURDAY. The photographer arrives, to stay till Monday, and take eleven photos: Mantlepiece, Gate-table, Comp. room, Office, Attics (2), Store-rooms, Garden, Frontage, View of house from Gardens, and the Staff. Sig. *b* of prelim. finished: prospectus put on.

OCTOBER 17 MONDAY. Photographer departs. Read sigs. NN and OO in first proof. Carpenter finishes shelves at bindery. Inspect sheet *b* of prelim.

OCTOBER 18 TUESDAY. 1000 prospectuses on 500 sheets finished. Lay them to dry in front room. Fold and cut a couple of hundred. At bindery, shift all quire-stock on to shelves and label: heavy work for one. Inspect second lot of vellum and turn out 44 sheets out of 500. LL put on.

OCTOBER 19 WEDNESDAY. Finish cutting and folding 1000 prospectuses. Lord Knollys replies to my letter regarding the dedication to the King, that his Majesty only accepts the dedications of works by authors with whom he is personally acquainted. I suppose his knowledge of Shakespeare is all second-hand.

OCTOBER 20 THURSDAY. Odd jobs: furniture and bedsteads: crockery arrives and is unpacked. Six barred chases arrive and six others sent off to be barred: also a set of inkers to the Durable Roller Co. A. C. Wyatt turns up on a visit. Inspect LL, and lay it out to dry, PP first proof and revise: QQ first proof: also slip proofs of booklet.

OCTOBER 21 FRIDAY. Read QQ: see Bailey about kitchen furniture; buy mattress, bolsters, and pillows. Inspect a retree ream, and select sheets for using on the prospectuses — 350 passable out of 500. The title-sheet is on the press, requiring 3 workings, two sides and the red line.

OCTOBER 22 SATURDAY. Title-sheet finished and layed out to dry in the dining room, with its vellums. Number the vellums. Inspect and count title-sheet. Wages and weekly accounts. Furniture from Bailey for kitchen.

OCTOBER 24 MONDAY. Start numbering the title-sheet on certificate. At odd times during a busy day do Nos. 1–700. Arrival of housekeeper, Mrs Holdich, and Palmer, bindery foreman. Busy with both, explaining and arranging stock. MM on machine.

OCTOBER 25 TUESDAY. Finished numbering title-sheet, and pack in hundreds. Clear dining room. Bailey round with furniture. A.H.B. arrives to stay till the end of the week in the S.H.P. Dine with him, inaugurating the dining room, and the Pebworth table. Sleep at lodgings. NN on machine.

OCTOBER 26 WEDNESDAY. A.H.B. interviews Bailey, and secures furniture. Open an account at Lloyds Bank. Notify postmaster of the existence of . . . . .
THE SHAKESPEARE HEAD PRESS, which we now call ourselves: subterfuges at an end.

Rushing about all day; carrying what are known as personal effects from lodgings to S.H.P.; fitting up attic as bedroom; putting outer of NN on; tasting various brews of beer to select a cask; arranging things at bindery; objurgating Cook, who chooses this busy day to make a more conspicuous ass of himself than ever before. OO on machine.

Begin to inhabit the S.H.P.

OCTOBER 27 THURSDAY. Order form in hand in three shapes, one for vellum copies, one for the booksellers, one for private customers. Also a trade notice. Head a few sheets with our title. A.H.B. busy with prospective arrangements. Odds and ends again all day. 2nd revises of final sheets of vol. I.

Composition of vol. II begun – the *Comedy of Errors*. At this point we alter the gauge of the sticks, including the numbering-column, which has hitherto been added in proof. Thus each page will be solid and secure in itself, and absolute register of side-figures ensured. It entails a new supply of leads for spacing: order these and a lead-cutter.

Speak to Pickworth, having decided (i) not to put him into the bindery, as he suggested (see Oct. 10), but (ii) to dismiss Cook, and offer him foreman's place. However, he prefers to remain compositor, and to introduce one Summerton, a friend, now foreman–newsman on the *Courier* at Leamington. Agree, and wire to Summerton to interview me tomorrow night.

OCTOBER 28 FRIDAY. PP put on machine, after various odd jobs – we have 3 different order forms on hand, a trade notice, and the booklet. Blocks arrive for the latter; A.H.B. and I finally arrange the copy for it. H. Morgan of Burn's and Dr Robertson Nicol expected as our guests. Mr Summerton calls in answer to my wire of yesterday: we engage him as foreman in Cook's place from Nov. 15th at 34/- a week. Morgan and Dr Nicol arrive; dine quatuor at the Shakespeare Hotel and sit up smoking and talking at the S.H.P. Send prospectus to Marie Corelli.

OCTOBER 29 SATURDAY. Marie Corelli subscribes for one copy, sends her cheque, and a kindly letter, to which I reply in kindly kind. Pay in cheques, give Cook a fortnight's warning; wages and weekly accounts. Inspect bindery with Morgan and make arrangements.

OCTOBER 31 MONDAY. Dr Nicol has made the astonishing proposal to A.H.B. to print Marie Corelli's works in an *edition de luxe*, and is strongly convinced it would be a great success. This is to be further discussed. At present I am strongly against it. Prospectuses issued to London papers and Stratford municipal authorities. Jobs on the machine, as PP is finished and QQ not back.

NOVEMBER 1 TUESDAY. Jobs again: order forms and pulls of booklet and heading note-paper. Send out 30 or 40 more prospectuses to newspapers, as per list from A.H.B. Jobs of envelope-heading; gummed-labels, and compliment-forms given out to Stanton and Stanley, local printers. Put up an electric bell from dining room to kitchen.

NOVEMBER 2 WEDNESDAY. Last 3 sheets, QQ, RR, SS, returned for press. Put QQ on. Odd jobs with order forms and prospectus. Sidney Lee calls with Lionel Cust. Dine with them at the Shakespeare Hotel.

NOVEMBER 3 THURSDAY. RR put on. Business with prospectus-envelopes, order forms inserted in prospectuses. Try to see the Henley St cottage with Sidney Lee, but cannot spare the time. See the cellar at the Birthplace, however, while being inspected with regard to fire-appliances. A.H.B. to interview girl for bindery – but she does not arrive. Evening: call on Marie Corelli.

NOVEMBER 4 FRIDAY. More kitchen furniture arrives. Men engaged on fitting stove and sink in kitchen. RR finished, and last sheet SS put on. We shall finish printing vol. I on Monday. Notice of the Press in the *Herald*.

NOVEMBER 5 SATURDAY.
FINISH PRINTING VOL. I.
SS (last sheet) finished. Wages and a/cs. Bindery goods arrive. A.H.B. for weekend.

NOVEMBER 7 MONDAY. The S.H.P. booklet put on the press. Engineer from Esson's arrives to investigate cause of rub on inkers. The fault seems to be in the bearers, after all. He puts these right, but only trial will show if this is the root of the trouble. Bindery-girl cannot come. Advt. in *B'ham Dly Post*.

NOVEMBER 8 TUESDAY. Have talked over Nicol's scheme with A.H.B. The only thing to do appears to be to offer to form a company separate from the S.H.P. (but to include the publishing firm) for general printing, leading off with an *edition de luxe* of Marie Corelli's books. If Nicol will not consent, let him do his worst!

A.H.B. returns to London. Enquiries are beginning to come in, especially with reference to the vellum copies. All trade prospectuses now sent out. Send vellum sheets LL — end to bindery to dry.

NOVEMBER 9 WEDNESDAY. Enquiries *re* vellum copies: and various people seeking prospectuses. Insurance inspector calls. Advt for bindery-girl in *Birmingham Post*. One application to hand. Re-estimate lengths of the ten volumes in pages and sheets. Begin addressing envelopes to private English book-buyers. Inner forme of booklet finished, and outer put on.

NOVEMBER 10 THURSDAY. Address more envelopes. Vellum now all dry: repack the whole to await binding. Consult about engaging extra assistance at the bindery for the sewing of the booklet.

NOVEMBER 11 FRIDAY. Girl (Annie Pitcher) calls, for position as folder and collator. Engage her at 15/- for next week to help over the booklet. Only 2 replies received to our B'ham advt. All prospectus-envelopes now headed with our device and address.

NOVEMBER 12 SATURDAY. 2 vellum copies sold. Letter has arrived this week from Sir Edwin Durning Laurence, Bart., M.P., a notorious Baconian, who deduces from our specimen page that we are aware of the real significance of "Ca-caliban" = κακ-αλιβας. Wages and accounts. Notices in the papers. Cook leaves.

NOVEMBER 14 MONDAY. Booklet finished: cover put on. Trouble with forme, until Mr Summerton, the new foreman, arrives, and puts it right. Alarm, apparently unfounded, of chimney on fire at bindery. Palmer, girl (Miss Pitcher) and Bridger all at work folding booklet.

NOVEMBER 15 TUESDAY. Various demands for prospectuses. Booklet cover on machine. Binding presses and backing-machine arrived yesterday. Stick gummed address-labels on envelopes for America.

NOVEMBER 16 WEDNESDAY. Booklet well under weigh: some finished: 100 sent off (uncut) to A.H.B. I despair of getting a good bindery-woman locally, or even at Birmingham, as all seem to be engaged for the Christmas work. Advt in *Chronicle* today appears useful: Palmer says he thinks the advertiser is a woman from Burn's. Four more sheets of vol. II to read. Another order for a vellum copy to hand. Addressed envelopes arrive from London – Bibliographical Society (217): country gentlemen of Oxfordshire (148), Warwickshire (166) and Herefordshire (178).

NOVEMBER 17 THURSDAY. 5000 prospectuses on machine. Jacobi's criticisms thereon to hand, just too late. New housekeeper, Mrs Sharp, arrives. Gumming printed addresses on envelopes.

NOVEMBER 18 FRIDAY. Gumming addresses again. A.H.B. has engaged a Miss Webb for the bindery. Mr and Mrs Arthur Symons on a visit, boarding opposite at Lewis's – not the butchers', but the New Place boarding-house. A.H.B. arrives. Business. Arthur Symons looks in at night.

NOVEMBER 19 SATURDAY. Prospectus-work. 50 cases to hand. Send two copies of vol. I in flat quires to Morgan, with portraits and cases, for advance subscription-copies. Wages and weekly accounts.

NOVEMBER 21 MONDAY. Prospectuses: folding, cutting; folding and pressing; inserting order forms and booklet, putting in envelopes, stamping, gumming and posting.

Oxfordshire and Warwickshire done. Miss Webb, bindery-forewoman, arrives.

NOVEMBER 22 TUESDAY. Prospectuses as yesterday. Binding begins: folding sheets. Glue arrives. A.H.B. leaves early (in *snow*) taking the vellum sheets of vol. I with him.

NOVEMBER 23 WEDNESDAY. Prospectuses again. Machine not running, as no sheets to hand. Cooper assists at bindery; Redding assists me and the office-boy with prospectuses. List of English book-collectors and the Bibliographical Society circularised.

NOVEMBER 24 THURSDAY. Hard frost: gas-supply deficient, but luckily engine-supply all right, as two sheets of Vol. II are returned.
        BEGIN TO PRINT VOL. II.
Prospectuses again; but we await results of former lots, before dispatching more.

NOVEMBER 25 FRIDAY. Sig. B of vol. II finished. Job notice to booksellers run off. Sig. C put on. THE FIRST COPY (No. 1) BOUND UP. Dodge for using its own for end-papers successful. We now wait only for the tissues to face portrait. Hard frost still – gas in trouble again, but put right.

NOVEMBER 26 SATURDAY. Still cold and frosty. Vol. II well under weigh. Some prospectuses returned, the addressees having "Gone away: left no address." Wages and accounts. To town.

NOVEMBER 28 MONDAY. See A.H.B. and H. G. Webb at Great Russell Street. More orders and a cheque to hand. Return to Stratford. Another order and cheque there.

NOVEMBER 29 TUESDAY. More prospectuses out. Sheets B, C, and D finished. Take on a half-tone job for Stanton, the printer next door to the Five Gables. We shall want another compositor to keep up with the machine. Thaw today.

NOVEMBER 30 WEDNESDAY. Our advertised day of publication, but I fear we shall have no copies ready till late tomorrow, as the pressing-boards have not come. Another compositor is *not* wanted; but I engage a boy – Pickworth's son – for the bindery.

DECEMBER 1 THURSDAY. Monthly accounts all morning. Pressing-boards turn up at midday, but bound copies not sufficiently pressed by night, and must be left till tomorrow. Miller & Richard's representative calls. Job for Stanton on machine, and finished. F put on. Summoned for "allowing a chimney to be on fire" at the bindery. Palmer goes to defend: the chimney was *not* on fire!

> [CHIMNEY *on* FIRE. – *Frank Sidgwick,* who did not appear, was summoned for allowing a chimney to be on fire at 7, Church-street on November 14th. – P.c. Workman proved the case, and a fine of 1s, and 4s costs, was inflicted.]

DECEMBER 2 FRIDAY. Bullen forwards a letter from Sidney Lee, written formally as Chairman of the Trustees of Shakespeare's Birthplace; Savage, our neighbour at New Place next door, has been complaining to them of the noise of our engine. See him, and consider what is to be done. Reply to Lee.

Bound copies to hand. Invoice, pack and send out the first lot on order. Binding going ahead strongly. Proofs. See Sutton's agent, to discover the cheapest way of dispatching parcels. Sig. F finished. G put on. A long and worrying day.

DECEMBER 3 SATURDAY. Hughes, of Sherratt & Hughes, Manchester, who has subscribed for a vellum copy, writes offering £75 cash down. Accept. New pulley arrives, and is put on. Order from Sotheran for one copy. Wages and accounts.

DECEMBER 5 MONDAY. Cornish of Birmingham wants to know price of a vellum copy. Revise of N to hand. H put on machine. A.H.B. arrives. Call on Savage, who is out: arrange to call tomorrow with Esson, the printer's outfitter, who is coming down. Write offering copies to Memorial Library and Town Library.

DECEMBER 6 TUESDAY. Re-consider for the Xth time the division of the plays into ten volumes, and draw out a scheme to keep vol. II rather small – four plays – in order to get it out quickly. First proofs of O. John Esson arrives. After lunch, and all the afternoon, trying to reduce noise and disturbance next door. Much attempted, something done. Savage amenable. Consult Esson about another machine; he suggests rearrangement of machine room to take a Wharfdale (cylinder) machine, as well as our Mitre. He stays overnight.

DECEMBER 7 WEDNESDAY. Esson about his business: A.H.B. off to Birmingham. Convoy Esson: he has been to see the Savages. He departs at midday. Get off the Memorial Library copy. A.H.B. brings another order from Birmingham, making four today.

DECEMBER 8 THURSDAY. A.H.B. to town early. Despatching copies: and a box of 50 to London. Pay in cheques: visit new Town Library, still in chaotic state, and leave them their vol. I. We are giving No. 1 to the Birthplace, No. 2 to the Memorial Library, and No. 3 to the Town Library. K put on.

Just before closing, Cooper calls me down to the machine room, and points out an ominous and dangerous vibration in the engine. We cannot fiddle about any longer, and must run slow or stop till we can get it properly bedded.

DECEMBER 9 FRIDAY. Busy all day arranging with engineer, builder, etc., to put engine outside in a shed of its own, and run shafting through the wall: we should have done this at first.

DECEMBER 10 SATURDAY. Engine and machine running at reduced speed: sig. L on. Wages and accounts.

DECEMBER 12 MONDAY. Having acted *re* gas-engine on my own responsibility, it is a relief to find A.H.B. approves: estimate of engineering to hand – £27.10.

DECEMBER 13 TUESDAY. Two more orders for vellum copies to hand through A.H.B., and Sherratt & Hughes's cheque for £75. Send Jacobi his presentation copy with a letter. Mudie's complain their copy has a faulty sheet. Accounts all afternoon.

DECEMBER 14 WEDNESDAY. Revise of R out: O returned for press. Mudie's copy returned, restored and returned again. Finish accounts to date.

DECEMBER 15 THURSDAY. N finished: O put on. First proofs of S and T: P and Q returned for press.

DECEMBER 16 FRIDAY. The shed for the gas-engine is now well on its way. In piercing the thick foundations of the machine-room for the shafting, it was found to be a double (hollow) wall, and BONES were found in the cavity. It remains to be seen whose bones they are!

DECEMBER 17 SATURDAY. Sig. P finished. Wages and weekly accounts. Arthur Symons' article in the *Speaker*.

DECEMBER 19 MONDAY. *No* correspondence in the morning! One letter later. The lack of orders is disheartening, and it won't get better this year. Sig. T out, and U in first proof. Dull slack day.

DECEMBER 20 TUESDAY. Blocks lent to the *World's Work*. Machine idle after midday. Q finished. U out for revise.

DECEMBER 21 WEDNESDAY. Press-proofs R and S returned: R put on at once. Lee's reply to our letter informing him and Trustees of steps taken to relieve Savage of vibration of gas-engine.

DECEMBER 22 THURSDAY. R finished. S put on. X sent out.

DECEMBER 23 FRIDAY. Y proofed and sent out. S finished. Rollers returned. Clearing up.

DECEMBER 24 SATURDAY. Holidays begin: machine stopped: composition going on.

DECEMBER 25–27 Holidays.

DECEMBER 28 WEDNESDAY. A.H.B. writes that Lippincott's refuse to take the Shakespeare at our price (half-price *net*), at least until they have gone into the matter more carefully, which Ridings, their representative, proposes to do in March next. All very well, but delays are dangerous.

When the engine is moved to the new shed, we shall want a stove of some kind in the machine-room. T put on.

DECEMBER 29 THURSDAY. T finished. U put on. First proofs and revise of Z sent out.

DECEMBER 30 FRIDAY. Prospectuses etc. to the Clark Co. of Cleveland, Ohio. Marie Corelli calls, and brings her landlord J. C. Tregarthen, a native of Stratford now departed, to view the works. He subscribes for a copy. M.C. tells me of a dialogue between the vicar (G. Arbuthnot) and my office-boy (M.C.'s butler's son). *The Vicar*: "Well, so you are in a printing-office? H'm, you won't sell any Shakespeares here: we don't want him." *My office boy*: "We don't provide for Stratford, sir."

The S.H.P. Christmas Supper takes place in the evening at the "Falcon." Male staff all present, with Messrs Stanton, Stanley, Bridger, and a Mr Hyman (pianist) present. Successful evening.

DECEMBER 31 SATURDAY. X on machine: first proofs of AA. Wages and weekly accounts.

1905

JANUARY 2 MONDAY. Prosit! Accounts all morning – monthly, quarterly, yearly. X finished off, the last sheet in hand.

JANUARY 3 TUESDAY. Visit of A.S., C.S.S., E.S.,* and Lady Trevelyan, with whom they are staying. She orders a copy. Inspection of the works. The machine room in disorder, as it is the beginning of the transit of the engine, and re-arrangement of the machine room. 1st proofs BB.

JANUARY 4 WEDNESDAY. Engine moved to shed. At the opening of the Free Library the S.T.‡ Shakespeare was the 2nd book taken out, selected by Sir George Trevelyan. Visit from Sidney Lee.

JANUARY 5 THURSDAY. Shafting fixed and machine turned round in machine room. Stove put in – gives great heat. 1st proofs of CC. Redding ill.

JANUARY 6 FRIDAY. Proofs pulled for London on machine by hand. Engine fixed and run. First proofs DD.

JANUARY 7 SATURDAY. Shafting connected up, belt to engine fixed, engine run for a few minutes – beautifully steady. All pipes fixed underground. Sir George Trevelyan pays up, and £50 from von Sobbe on account for his vellum copy. Wages and balancing. More paper to hand.

JANUARY 9 MONDAY. Marie Corelli sends in two orders from friends of hers. Machine belted up, and running again. Y put on, inner finished. Redding still ill,; he turns up but I send him home.

JANUARY 10 TUESDAY. Y finished, Z put on. EE to London.

* *Arthur Sidgwick: the writer's father.*
Charlotte Sophia Sidgwick: the writer's mother.
Ethel Sidgwick: the writer's sister.
‡ *Stratford Town.*

JANUARY 11 WEDNESDAY. Signed order from one of M.C.'s friends. Cheque as well: also from A.S. for his second copy. BB and CC returned for press.

JANUARY 12 THURSDAY. Folding, cutting, folding prospectuses, inserting order form and booklet, and putting up in envelopes for America: private book-buyers and universities, colleges and schools. AA put on. First proofs of GG, beginning *A Midsummer Night's Dream*.

JANUARY 13 FRIDAY. Prospectuses to America finished off. First proofs of HH. Work on engine shed ending: painting, boxing-in shafting, etc.

JANUARY 14 SATURDAY. Despondent letter from A.H.B. but another order to hand. Wages and accounts. Have touched up some of the broken letters in vol. I, sig. CC.

JANUARY 16 MONDAY. More paper to hand. A.H.B. down: inspects engine shed and machine room: discuss ways and means, and plan of campaign. Calculations as to cost of production per vol. and the whole.

JANUARY 17 TUESDAY. DD put on. HH to London. Continue touching up CC in vol. I.

JANUARY 18 WEDNESDAY. FF returned for press. 1st proofs II. Write to Mrs Drummond for an introduction to her brother F. R. Benson.

JANUARY 19 THURSDAY. Sig. EE finished. Vellum sheets B–O of vol. II sent to be dried at bindery.

JANUARY 20 FRIDAY. Design a hanging-sign for the outside of the S.H.P. Show-case, also for outside wall, put in hand. FF put on.

JANUARY 21 SATURDAY. Vellum sheets of B–O dried: send P–EE to be dried. Letter from F. R. Benson. Wages and weekly accounts.

JANUARY 23 MONDAY. A.H.B. down, with Mr Carruthers Miller, of the Riverside Press, Edinburgh – a possible assistant and manager. Mr Fox of No. 1, High Street (the Shakespeare–Quiney house) calls to make acquaintance. First order from America to hand.

JANUARY 24 TUESDAY. 3rd instalment of vellum arrives. Sort it through in the morning. GG finished: HH put on. Proof of LL to London.

JANUARY 25 WEDNESDAY. II back for press just in time. First proofs MM. Call Welcombe aft.

JANUARY 26 THURSDAY. A.H.B. wants me to take his place at the Eliz. dinner tomorrow night. I can get away by putting on title-sheet to vol. II next. Put this in hand. II on machine.

JANUARY 27 FRIDAY. II finished: Title put on. Wages paid. Away till Monday.

JANUARY 30 MONDAY. In my absence, they have managed to make a mistake in the title-sheet. It is imposed so that when folded the blank comes as the fourth leaf instead of the first. This we shall have to correct in binding by cutting it through the head and turning it back, and then sewing double. Benson's people say that the advt matter on programmes is not in their hands, but in those of the Memorial committee.

JANUARY 31 TUESDAY. KK finished, MM returned for press. First proofs of OO. Vol. II ends conveniently with sig. PP. New housekeeper arrives.

FEBRUARY 1 WEDNESDAY. Monthly accounts. Financial crisis approaching: A.H.B. negotiating in London. Report that Sir Henry Irving is to open the Memorial Week on Easter Monday with *The Merchant of Venice*.

FEBRUARY 2 THURSDAY. NN returned for press. MM put on. Mrs Sharpe goes. Monthly accounts squared with pass-book. PP to London. Copy not to hand: start *Merchant of Venice* from other copy for vol. III.

FEBRUARY 3 FRIDAY. The Press is getting into financial straits. The trouble is to tide over till March, when the American sales ought to be fixed up. Interview Birmingham art student, Sanders, *re* signboard.

FEBRUARY 4 SATURDAY. OO returned for press. NN finished. First proofs of vol. III. Wages and weekly balancings.

FEBRUARY 6 MONDAY. OO put on. 2nd proofs B, 1st proofs C, of vol. III.

FEBRUARY 7 TUESDAY. OO finished, and PP not yet returned: machine idle after 10.30. A.H.B. has sold another copy.

FEBRUARY 8 WEDNESDAY. First proofs D. PP vol. II returned and put on. Vellums to be dried. Sidney Lee.

FEBRUARY 9 THURSDAY. B returned for press and put on. Second proof D: first E. Show-case to hang outside arrives and is fixed in position, with prospectus and volume in it. Attracts much attention and comments. Looks very neat. C returned for press.

FEBRUARY 10 FRIDAY. Vellum of vol. II now all dried. Pack carefully in box for delivery to Webb, who binds the vellum copies. E to London. C put on.

FEBRUARY 11 SATURDAY. Morgan writes for bulk-copy of vol. 2 to make cases. Send it off. C finished 12.0. and D not back. We shall quicken up next week, as new compositor comes on Monday.

FEBRUARY 13 MONDAY. New compositor W. H. Wesson arrives. Miss Pitcher leaves bindery. D returned and put on. A.H.B. down. He means to see the Shakespeare through, and develop the Press. To this end he proposes to appoint

Simpkin's our London agents, transfer most of the stock to them, come and live here himself, set me partly free to live in town and keep an eye on Simpkin's, and work away at our usual business here, giving up the London office altogether. First proofs F.

FEBRUARY 14 TUESDAY. D finished, E not back. Cooper idle of necessity half the day. First proofs G.

FEBRUARY 15 WEDNESDAY. E, returned late last night, put on the press. First proofs H. We can turn out a sheet a day now from the comp. room. Cooper takes just over a day to work a sheet: we shall thus gradually draw ahead of him.

FEBRUARY 16 THURSDAY. E finished, and F not back, so Cooper is again idle of necessity. Waiting the signature all day. First proofs I, revised and sent to London. F returned at night.

FEBRUARY 17 FRIDAY. G returned. First proofs K. F on machine.

FEBRUARY 18 SATURDAY. G put on. K to London. Wages and accounts.

FEBRUARY 20 MONDAY. H and I returned for press. This relieves anxiety, and we ought to keep moving all right now.

FEBRUARY 21 TUESDAY. Another order (C.C.L.)* and cheque to hand. First proofs of *As You Like it*. M to London.

FEBRUARY 22 WEDNESDAY. Cases for vol. I to hand: but none for vol. II, and we are waiting for them. K returned. N to London.

FEBRUARY 23 THURSDAY. Experiment with sonnet on the principle of one-to-a-page. K put on. O to London.

FEBRUARY 24 FRIDAY. First and second proofs P. L returned and put on. Bulk-copy vol. II returned cased.

* *C.C.L., if I read this correctly, would be C. C. Lynam, Headmaster at Dragon School, Oxford.*

FEBRUARY 25 SATURDAY. Another delivery of paper to hand. 100 of vol. II sewn ready for casing, but no cases and no frontispieces ready yet. First and second proofs Q. Wages and accounts.

FEBRUARY 27 MONDAY. Mr Nigel Bond, secretary of the National Trust for Preservation of Ancient Buildings and Natural Beauties (etc.) and a prospective partner in the S.H.P. comes on a visit of inspection. The Duke of Devonshire intends to subscribe. Suggest a vellum copy.

FEBRUARY 28 TUESDAY. Routine. Some of Esson's chases giving trouble again. A sheet a day is our comp.'s average.

MARCH 1 WEDNESDAY. Cases still delayed for vol. 2. A.H.B. is completing arrangements by which he will come to Stratford at the end of the month, and I shall retire to the metropolis.

MARCH 2 THURSDAY. Gas escaping in machine room. Set to rights. O finished. Chases jumping and bowing. First proofs U.

MARCH 3 FRIDAY. R returned for press. Second proof U to London, first proofs X.

MARCH 4 SATURDAY. Specimen page for sonnets, imitating old-fashioned style with ornaments top and bottom. Pull sent off to A.H.B.

MARCH 6 MONDAY. A.H.B. down: approves of the sonnet page highly. Arrangements finally made for me to leave Stratford about the end of this month, when he comes down: overlapping Miller (see Jan. 23) who is engaged for half his time to be manager here. Discuss various projects.

MARCH 7 TUESDAY. Y to London: first proofs Z: Q finished, R put on. Sidney Lee visits us. Vol. II ISSUED: 25 copies bound.

MARCH 8 WEDNESDAY. Packing and sending out vol. II all morning. Proofs, etc. afternoon. Evening, set specimen page for Sidney's *Arcadia*, the projected first volume of "Shakespeare's Books".

MARCH 9 THURSDAY. Second proofs AA, first proof BB. T put on.

MARCH 10 FRIDAY. 50 copies vol. II off to A.H.B. in London. Second proofs BB, first CC: T finished, U put on.

MARCH 11 SATURDAY. Y returned for press. Specimen page for *Arcadia* pulled, and sent out with CC. Wages and weekly accounts. Give Palmer notice.

MARCH 13 MONDAY. Z returned. First proofs DD. X on machine.

MARCH 14 TUESDAY. We are sending out written applications to all the crowned heads of Europe, enclosing prospectuses, French and German. M. Loubet's secretary replies from Paris that there are too many similar applications to justify him acceding to ours, and permits himself the assurance of his profound respects.

MARCH 15 WEDNESDAY. A.H.B. is getting run down by the fatigue of this constant strain and the search for a financier. So far all have cried off. A loan from A.S.* relieves us temporarily; and A.H.B. expects, after recouping here awhile, to be able to find the man we want. No doubt the "season" will help us.

MARCH 16 THURSDAY. AA put on. First proofs GG, and FF to London. A.H.S.† for a night.

MARCH 17 FRIDAY. GG to London, first proofs HH, read to me by A.H.S.

MARCH 18 SATURDAY. Palmer to leave after next week, and the casing to be done in London. Wages and weekly accounts.

* *Arthur Sidgwick: father.*
† *Arthur Hugh Sidgwick: brother.*

54

MARCH 20 MONDAY. This appears to be my last week here. A.H.B. writes that he will be down on Thursday, and as he and his cousins will occupy the S.H.P. till the bindery is ready, I shall depart that day. So at least it is arranged at present.

MARCH 21 TUESDAY. Gorgeous spring weather: the garden is becoming quite ornamental. Packing various books and effects. Printing sheet of press notices.

MARCH 22 WEDNESDAY. Sore throat and catarrh giving a rheumy Finis.

MARCH 23 THURSDAY. Return to town.

as good as those for 1907 I shall
be more than satisfied. The "Collections"
were most interesting.

So poor old Ebsworth has gone
to his long home. I hadn't seen
him for years. He had intended
to leave his books (252 a very valuable
lot, I fancy) to St. John's Coll. Camb.
and it must have been a wrench
for him when he had to sell
them for his belly's needs.

[Private] I meditate printing a Defoe
in 200 volumes, at a guinea
a volume, strictly limited to
1500 copies.

£210

1500
____
£315,000

If it's well taken-up (and if
I vigorously keep down expenses) I
reckon there ought to be £200,000
profit in it. No petty piffling schemes
for me! but mum's the word.
Yours always A. H. Bullen

Portion of a letter by Bullen, date and recipient unknown.

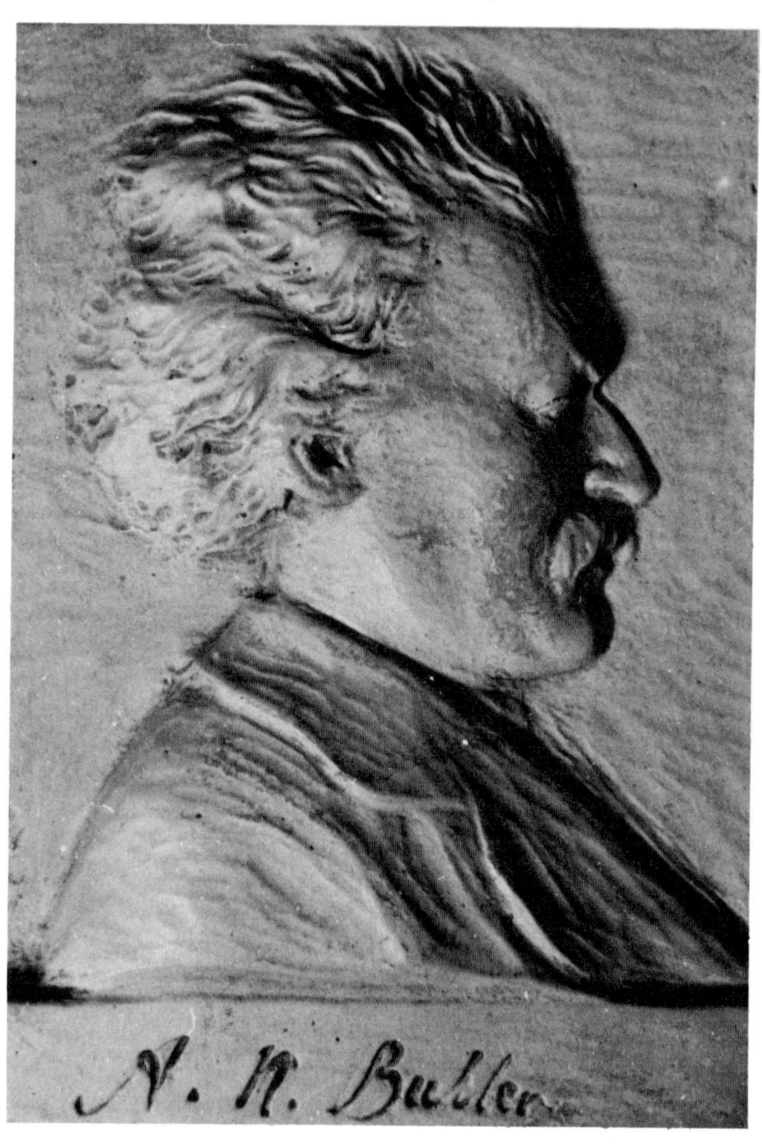

A. H. Bullen from a plaque, artist unknown

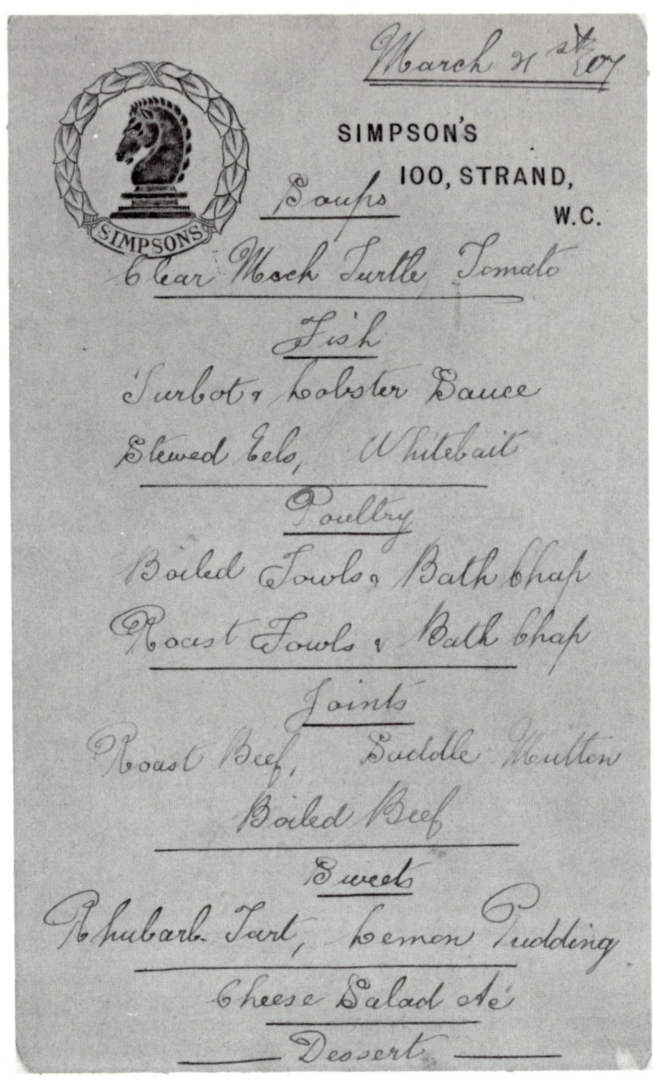

ABOVE Menu of dinner commemorating the completion of *The Stratford Town Shakespeare*. RIGHT Signatures of those attending the Commemorative Dinner – Arthur F. Wallis, Charles C. Tennant, R. B. McKerrow, A. W. Pollard, E. K. Chambers, W. W. Greg,

R. Warwick Bond, Otto Sullman, G. Thorn Drury, A. H. Bullen, A. Vian, Thomas Seccombe, E. V. Lucas, Gerald M. Bishop, C. R. Ashbee, A. Francis Sherrard, George H. Powell, Percy Spalding, Frank Pacy, Frank Sidgwick.

Frank Sidgwick, 1910

H. F. B. BRETT-SMITH'S FOREWORD TO SHAKESPEARE'S SONNETS

[After the death of A. H. Bullen in 1920 I was approached by his executors with the proposal that I should acquire his Shakespeare Head Press at Stratford-upon-Avon. For a year or two previously I had been making some modest attempts at fine printing, moved to it by the discovery of an article on the subject by Bernard Newdigate in a special number of *The Studio* of 1912 and encouraged by the generous guidance of Emery Walker.

The Press had, I believe, been in difficulties for some time, but its reputation for scholarly books, well printed, stood high. It seemed best to form a separate company, and so the Shakespeare Head Press Ltd was established by a small group of scholars and bibliophiles who shared the ideals of Bullen, and between them looked to replace competently the energy and enthusiasm of the versatile scholar of whom the DNB commemorates the "excellent literary intuition but small business capacity".

Bernard Newdigate was to design and print the books, H. F. B. Brett-Smith (later Goldsmith's Reader in English Literature at Oxford) was to safeguard their scholarship, and they were to be published from Oxford with the imprint of Basil Blackwell.

A few days before his death Bullen had passed for press a new edition of Shakespeare's Sonnets. The type was standing and it was resolved to print the book with a Foreword by Brett-Smith, giving an account of Bullen's life and work. Reading this again after many years, I deem it to be so excellent that it should be restored to print as part of this volume.   BASIL BLACKWELL]

FOREWORD TO THE SONNETS

IT IS little over a year since A. H. Bullen wrote the closing sentences of his last contribution to the study of Elizabethan literature. He was already more ill than he knew, and the Note appended to the present edition of Shakespeare's *Sonnets* was completed in pencil (hardly more than two pages of the MS. are in ink) by February 23, 1920. Six days later he died, leaving the text of the *Sonnets* already printed off under his direction, and only awaiting his final account of them.

That account is now printed, without addition or comment, from Bullen's MS. His first text of the *Sonnets* had appeared in 1905, with a five page Note written in May of that year. A second issue, without a Note, was printed in 1912.* In preparing the revised Note for the present edition, he worked at first upon that of May, 1905, and the two opening pages of his MS., written on leaves of an old note book, are co-extensive with the first two pages of the original Note, from which they differ hardly at all. Then there is a complete break, and the latter part of the Note, entirely re-written and altered from that of 1905, is continued in pencil on sheets of writing paper.

For the second issue, planned years before it appeared, Bullen's original intention had been not only to suppress his own Note, but to obtain an Introduction from Swinburne. Failing in this, he issued his plain text in 1912, and at length in 1920 revised his original work. The last letter in the collection of Swinburne's correspondence published in 1918 was addressed to Bullen on January 11, 1909, and contains this passage: "I should be glad to do anything which you would take as a personal compliment, but I could not undertake the task proposed. The best possible intro-

---

* I have not seen a copy of this issue, and my authority for the statement is Bullen's secretary, who has been good enough to read the proofs of this Foreword.

duction to the *Sonnets* was many years ago prefixed by François Victor Hugo to his matchless and marvellous translation of them. You could not possibly, in my opinion, do better than get some competent scholar to send you by way of preface a close and careful version of it."

It would ill become the successors of Arthur Henry Bullen to issue his final work without making some public acknowledgement of the debt which is due to him alike from English literature and English scholarship. He had them both in his blood, for his father, George Bullen, C.B., LL.D., was for many years Keeper of Printed Books at the British Museum, and the habit of scholarship was ingrained; as early as 1884 we find the son declaring in print that "the loss of an arm or a leg would be a slight price for a genuine student to pay if only he could discover one new fact about Shakespeare's history"!* A. H. Bullen was educated at the City of London School, and went up as an Open Classical Scholar to Worcester College, Oxford, where he took a First in Classical Mods. in 1877, a Third in Greats in 1878, and the degree of B.A. in 1879. It is not improbable that the magnificent collection of seventeenth-century literature in Worcester College Library may have done its work in forming his early tastes, and we know that Swinburne's studies on Ford and Chapman did for him something of what Charles Lamb did for Swinburne himself as a boy at Eton.† At any rate, although Bullen occupied himself for some time after leaving Oxford in preparing pupils for the Universities and Public Schools, his interest in the chosen period was shown almost immediately, for his seven volume‡ edition of the Works of John Day was completed as early as 1881.

In this decade, 1881–90, Bullen produced an astonishing amount of valuable work. Of the Elizabethan and seven-

* Preface to Paltock's *Peter Wilkins*.

† Swinburne's letter to Bullen of June 19, 1882.

‡ They may be called "volumes", as they were separately paged, but "parts" would better represent their bulk.

teenth century dramatists he edited not only Day, but Marlowe,* Middleton, Marston, Nabbes, Peele and Davenport, besides the anonymous play *Arden of Feversham,* and the sixteen pieces in the four annual volumes of *Old English Plays* (1882–5). All these books were published, or privately printed, in limited editions, and their direct influence on the mass of the general public was to that extent reduced, but their effect was far-reaching in that they made readable and accessible many Elizabethan plays which were hard to obtain, and some which were unobtainable. A privately printed edition of 150 copies† is robbed of some of its efficacy, but it can at any rate reach the leaders, and Swinburne voiced the opinion of the enthusiast when he wrote on October 8, 1882: "I know no books of their kind better edited than your *Old English Plays,* including the Works of John Day; and I trust these are but the first-fruits of a noble harvest yet to be gathered in. I am eagerly awaiting the promised second volume of your collection."

For any ordinary man this would have been ample occupation for ten years. But Bullen did not neglect his other great interest, the lyric, and he produced within the same period his volume of selections from Drayton (selections which Swinburne thought "could not have been better made"); his edition of that exquisite and forgotten lyric poet Thomas Campion; his Christmas Garland of *Carols and Poems*; his reprints of the two Elizabethan Song-Books named *England's Helicon* (1600) and Davison's *Poetical Rhapsody* (1602); and his own world-famous anthologies, *Lyrics* (with its second volume of *More Lyrics*) *from the Song-Books of the Elizabethan Age, Lyrics from Elizabethan Dramatists, Lyrics from Elizabethan Romances,* and the love poems of *Musa Proterva* and *Speculum Amantis*. These volumes, known

---

* This contained the best-known example of Bullen's acuteness as a textual critic; his interpretation of the mysterious "Oncaymaeon" of *Dr. Faustus,* I. i. 12, which had baffled all previous editors, as the Aristotelian ὄν καὶ μὴ ὄν.

† This was the form in which Day and the *Old English Plays* (the second series of which included Nabbes and Davenport) appeared.

61

wherever the English tongue is spoken, are their own best praise; they comprise a body of early lyric unmatched for beauty and variety, and they include many waifs rescued from forgotten print, like Captain Tobias Hume's "Fain would I change that note To which fond love hath charmed me," or discovered in such unpublished MSS. as that in the Library of Christ Church from which Bullen drew the fine verses "Yet if his majesty our sovereign lord.'*

Even this tale does not exhaust the output of that marvellous decade, for during it he contributed articles to the *Dictionary of National Biography*, chiefly on English Literature of the sixteenth and seventeenth centuries, which enabled Leslie Stephen to "say with great confidence that his knowledge of that period is very remarkable, and, in some respects, probably unsurpassed." And there are still a few miscellaneous books to record: editions of Paltock's extraordinary romance of *Peter Wilkins*; of Izaak Walton's *Lives*; of a namesake William Bullein's *Dialogue against the Feuer Pestilence*, 1578, published by the Early English Text Society; and of the first volume of a pamphlet-series of "Ancient Drolleries", *Cobbes Prophecies*, 1614. This series, like much of the earlier work, was insufficiently supported by the public,† and it came to an end with the second volume, *Pimlyco*, in 1891.‡ Bullen had made unsuccessful application in 1889 for the Chair of English Language and Literature at University College, London; he found himself without prospect of that usual reward of the English scholar, the honourable poverty of one of our greater Universities; he had learned the bitter lesson that scholarship is not a com-

* Among Bullen's services in this field may also be reckoned the publication in 1907 of the valuable collection of *Early English Lyrics* chosen by Mr E. K. Chambers and Mr Frank Sidgwick, who very appropriately dedicated it to him.

† The *Old English Plays*, however, were in great demand from the beginning though he had printed too few copies to derive material benefit from this.

‡ I am informed on good authority that No. 3, *Quips upon Questions*, was printed but never issued, and that it was announced as having "appeared" in Lawrence and Bullen's catalogue of Autumn, 1896.

62

mercial asset, and yet with undaunted valour he turned publisher in earnest, and by the sheer excellence of his books caused the public to support good literature. In the twelve years from 1891 to 1902 Bullen wrote little himself – introductions to an edition of Anacreon with Thomas Stanley's translation, to *The Anatomy of Melancholy*, and to the Poems of William Browne – but the firm of Lawrence and Bullen published a great deal of admirable work. Few book-lovers do not feel a thrill at the sight of the familiar peacock blue and gold of the original issue of the Muses' Library, with its editions of such poets as Blake and Gay and Marvell, Drummond and Henry Vaughan, Herrick and Waller, John Donne, Thomas Carew and William Browne. The policy of the "limited edition" was given up, except for large paper copies, and an attempt was made to interest existing book-lovers, and train new ones, by genuine good work. The editors and writers of introductions were sometimes poets of the standing of Swinburne or Mr W. B. Yeats, sometimes scholars of repute, among whom were Mr G. Thorn Drury, Mr E. K. Chambers, Mr W. C. Ward, G. A. Aitken, H. C. Beeching and Mr George Saintsbury. The series was an undoubted success, and Mr Robert Bridges's introduction to Keats was so good that a separate issue was printed.

There was also another series, of not less merit, begun in the Lawrence and Bullen period.* This consisted of translations of the acknowledged classics of early Italian and French prose fiction, Boccaccio, Masuccio, Straparola, Ser Giovanni and Rabelais; it was worthily printed and illustrated, and the books are good to handle and to read.†

* Bullen left the firm of Lawrence and Bullen about 1900. Mr. Frank Sidgwick joined him in October 1901, becoming a partner six months later. They published first in Cecil Court, Charing Cross Road, and afterwards at 47, Great Russell Street, always under the style of A. H. Bullen, until March, 1907, when the partnership was dissolved. Mr Sidgwick retained the Great Russell Street business until October, 1908, when the present company of Sidgwick and Jackson was founded. During the first ten months of the Shakespeare Head Press, from May, 1904, to March, 1905, Mr Sidgwick was at Stratford, and Bullen remained in London; thereafter they changed places.

† The translation of *The Decameron* was by John Payne, but a new one by

In 1903 Bullen returned for a moment to anthologies, and wrote introductions for the volumes of *Shorter* and *Longer Elizabethan Poems* in *The English Garner*. But he was now fired with the ambition to print and publish a great edition of Shakespeare's Complete Works in the poet's native town, and for this purpose he acquired a lease of the house of Julius Shaw, the friend of Shakespeare and the first witness to his will. In this house, which has ever since been its home, Bullen founded the Shakespeare Head Press, and here from 1904 to 1907, two doors to the north of New Place, the type of the ten volumes of the Stratford Town Shakespeare was composed by Stratford men.

The successful completion of this great undertaking,* to which several experts contributed, is the more remarkable in that Bullen was engaged at the same time on a Variorum text of Beaumont and Fletcher, which he published jointly with Messrs George Bell & Sons. This edition was to have been completed in twelve volumes, of which only four appeared (in 1904–5–8–12); but among its editors were Mr W. W. Greg, Dr R. B. McKerrow, Mr E. K. Chambers and Mr P. A. Daniel, and it is regrettable that a really valuable text of Beaumont and Fletcher should remain unfinished.

Bullen's literary history after his migration to Stratford is chiefly the history of the Shakespeare Head Press. This was not his only interest, for he also published elsewhere, and one of his greatest books, Dr McKerrow's edition of Nashe, was printed in Oxford and issued from Great Russell Street.† There were other adventures too, and we have it on "Kather-

J. M. Rigg, with the same illustrations, was issued later (in 1903) in a smaller size, and uniform with it (in 1904) a new issue of the Urquhart and Motteux *Rabelais* in three volumes (the earlier one had been in two).

* Bullen's part in the work is more important than the mere extent of his fifty-odd pages of "Brief notes on the Text" might suggest. They contain valuable matter, and among his emendations the reading "mates the senses vouch" for the corrupt "makes the senses rough" of 1 *Henry VI*, v, iii, 70–1, has been singled out for well-deserved applause.

† Vols. i and ii, 1904, vol. iii, 1905, vol. iv, 1908. Vol. v, 1910, has the imprint of Messrs Sidgwick and Jackson.

64

ine Tynan's" authority that "he was most happily at home during the good year* when he edited *The Gentleman's Magazine* for Lord Northcliffe". But in general the Shakespeare Head Press absorbed his time, and he gave up to the encouragement and help of his authors and editors, and to the practical and necessary details of a publisher's office, much of the eager energy which had enabled him to produce alone† four dozen volumes between the years 1881 and 1890. In some ways this is regrettable; the "dream‡ of following the Stratford Town Shakespeare by editions of all the Elizabethan dramatists" was unfulfilled, though a certain amount of preliminary work had been carried through. But in other ways literature benefited by his unselfishness. The publications of the Shakespeare Head Press are no negligible contribution to the cause of good scholarship and good printing in England. They include, in original writing, the eight volumes of the Collected Works of Mr W. B. Yeats,§ selected by the poet and containing much otherwise unprocurable matter. In criticism, there are the scholarly papers in the volumes of Mr Charles Crawford's *Collectanea*, and of

* 1906. The sub-editor was Dr McKerrow. Miss Tynan adds: "I doubt if there was ever as good a magazine as that while it lasted." *Bookman*, April, 1920. The period of Bullen's editorship was from February to the end of the year. He ran the magazine somewhat on the old lines, with a view to readers who were not mere specialists but took a cultivated interest in antiquities generally; and for such a public he undoubtedly did excellent work. He enforced anonymity, but wrote himself in the paper and collected good contributors, and he was conscious of having found at last exactly the post for which he was fitted. The magazine was gradually becoming known, and his severance from it at the end of 1906 was a blow from which he never entirely recovered.

† "Alone" is used in no narrow sense; Bullen had valuable help from Professor C. H. Firth, F. G. Fleay and others. But none the less his issues of 1881–90 were an Atlantean task.

‡ A writer in the *Bookman's Journal*, March 12, 1920, states that Bullen spoke to him of such a project in 1917.

§ From the earliest days Bullen had confidence in Mr Yeats' work and gave him generous help and championship. No notice of Bullen would be complete without some mention also of his long-standing friendship with George Gissing, perhaps the only novelist whom he really admired.

Mr W. J. Lawrence's *The Elizabethan Playhouse*; and among editions of older English authors there is the admirable work of Professor G. C. Moore Smith on Gabriel Harvey, and Mr Montague Summers' *The Rehearsal*, and his six volumes of the Plays of Aphra Behn. A full list of the valuable books issued would be tedious and unnecessary; it is enough to claim for Bullen's publications the benefit of his ripe judgement and his remarkable knowledge.

Bullen had long come to his own as a scholar and outlived the early neglect of some of his work; the "systematic injustice and apparent envy or malevolence"* of his early reviewers could no longer affect his position. When he died he had been for some years in enjoyment of a Civil List Pension conferred on him by his old schoolfellow and contemporary at Oxford, Mr H. H. Asquith. More valuable than this was the universal respect of English scholars. As early as 1889 his position had been recognised by good judges at home and abroad; Swinburne and John Addington Symonds had borne witness to his ability both in research and in appreciative criticism; M A. Beljame had acknowledged the value "non seulement de son savoir, mais aussi de son jugement littéraire, aussi sûr que délicat'; M J. J. Jusserand had welcomed the *Collection of Old English Plays* as "surely the best addition made since the far-off days of Dodsley to our store of inedited plays"; and Delius in 1884 had lectured on one of them, the tragedy of Sir John Van Olden Barnavelt, in Berlin. Later tributes were not wanting, and we need only quote Dr McKerrow's acknowledgement in the final volume of his Nashe, "To Mr Bullen indeed the existence of the edition, which was first proposed to me by him, is entirely due." Those who are acquainted with that fine piece of Elizabethan scholarship should not forget, in their gratitude to the editor, their gratitude to his publisher and prompter.†

* Swinburne's letter to Bullen of July 10–24, 1885, on the reception of his Middleton.

† One other example of the same kind is too important for omission. To

66

And with all this, Bullen had the modesty of the true scholar. He knew indeed, and did not hesitate to proclaim, the value of what he had done. He wrote in the preface to his fourth volume of *Old English Plays*, "I may be pardoned for regarding the Collection with some pride. Six of the sixteen plays are absolutely new, printed for the first time; and I am speaking within bounds when I declare that no addition so substantial has been made to the Jacobean drama since the days of Humphrey Moseley and Francis Kirkman." But he knew also, as every scholar does, the inevitable limitations of even the best work, and he did not always succeed in satisfying his own high standard. With his Marston, in particular, he was never content, and even before his edition of that difficult author appeared he spoke of it as "the most laborious and irritating work that ever I undertook".*

Since Bullen's prime there has been some change in the methods of English scholarship; the demands made upon editors are more exacting; science has invaded the domain of literature, and it would be impossible now for the expert to do justice to an output which Bullen, working untiringly but on the broader lines of his day, was able to produce. But the aesthetic value of his books to all lovers of English literature is unimpaired, and no juster tribute has yet been paid to the man than that which Mr Charles Whibley published only a few days after his death. "No man of his time has more profoundly studied or more wisely interpreted the literature of the Elizabethan age than he . . . He thought no pains excessive, if only he might correct a faulty reading or attain to a perfect accuracy . . . His ear was so carefully attuned to

Bullen also Elizabethan scholars owe Mr. W. W. Greg's three admirable volumes, *Henslowe's Diary* (1904–8) and *The Henslowe Papers* (1907), all of which he published. In the preface to the *Diary* Mr Greg writes: "Lastly my best thanks are due to my friend Mr. A. H. Bullen, who originally suggested to me the idea of the present edition, volunteering himself to undertake the publication, and further supplied many helpful suggestions during the course of the work."

* Letter of December 22, 1886, to Henry Daniel, the late Provost of Worcester, *penes me*.

the verse of his chosen period, his learning was so wide and so deep, that few will ever challenge the boldest of his ascriptions . . . Above all, he was a great discoverer. He brought to light from the old songs, printed or in manuscript, many an unknown treasure . . .

"He has won honour not only by the work which he did himself, but by the work which he inspired others to do. 'The Shakespeare Head Press', which he established at Stratford-on-Avon, claims for itself a place in history. There indeed, sentiment and scholarship joined hands. The house in which the press stood was of Shakespeare's time. A. H. Bullen, who managed it, was not merely a typographer; he was the master, as few are masters, of the lore which belonged to Shakespeare and his contemporaries. That he should have printed the works of Shakespeare not far from the place where their author spent the last years of his life was just and proper . . He achieved much, he planned much that he did not achieve, and he has left all those who care for the understanding of our English literature under a deep debt of gratitude. And I would that the press so long the object of his care and pride might still survive to carry out some of the plans which he cherished to the end."

It is the hope of the present directors of the Shakespeare Head Press that this aspiration may now be fulfilled. They are anxious that the Press should produce no work unworthy of its traditions, whether in scholarship or in printing; and it is with full appreciation of the handing on of the torch that they issue, as their first publication, the final word upon a literary problem of universal interest of the great scholar whom they succeed.

H. F. B. BRETT-SMITH

Oxford, April 1921.

ARTHUR HENRY BULLEN (1857–1920)
AND THE SHAKESPEARE HEAD PRESS*

by PAUL MORGAN

FEW PEOPLE today can remember much about A. H. Bullen
except that he was a pioneer in editing or writing about
minor Elizabethan authors – someone not in the first rank,
but rather a fringe type who managed to scrape into a
Dictionary of National Biography Supplement. I came to look
into his chequered and rather sad career through an interest
in printing firms in my native town of Stratford-upon-Avon.

His is a depressing story; to understand his character and
what he did it is necessary to know something of his origins
and early years, since he is a casebook example of the
influences of both heredity and environment. Bullen was the
second son of George Bullen, an Irishman from County
Cork, who migrated to London, first as a schoolmaster at
St Olave's, shortly afterwards moving to the staff of the
British Museum, where he eventually became Keeper of
Printed Books from 1875 to 1890, dying in 1894. This
Irish origin was an important factor in his son's later activi-
ties. George Bullen is chiefly known to us today as the man
behind the *Catalogue of Books in the Library of the British
Museum Printed in England, Scotland and Ireland . . . to the
year 1640*, which appeared in 1884, and on which he had
worked for a long time. This pioneer piece of work, the real
basis of the Bibliographical Society's *Short-Title Catalogue*
of 1926, brought him into contact with all the literature of
the period, great and small, which fascinated the son so
greatly and to which, I cannot help feeling, he was intro-
duced by his father.

* This account is based on a lecture given to the Birmingham Bibliographical
Society, and also to the Northern Group of the Printing Historical Society,
both in October 1972, and amended in the light of subsequent discoveries,
such as Frank Sidgwick's Diary.

Arthur Henry Bullen attended the City of London School, then in Cheapside, under the headmastership of Edwin Abbott, the philologist, whose publications include a *Shakespearian Grammar*, printed in 1870, when Bullen was 13, and work on Francis Bacon. Abbott is known to have instilled a love of Elizabethan literature into his pupils, so here was an influence complementing that of George Bullen. It was significant for Bullen junior that there were also boys at this school who later became well known; the oldest was H. H. Asquith, there from 1863 to 1870, and Prime Minister in due course, who comes into the story. There were also two boys to be mentioned both two years his junior: H. C. Beeching, Dean of Norwich and a writer on Shakespeare, who contributed an essay to Bullen's ten volume Shakespeare printed in Stratford; and Solomon Lazarus Lee, who changed his forename to Sidney in 1890. Lee later got Bullen to write some biographies for the *DNB*, but the friendship ended some time after Bullen settled in Stratford, for reasons I have not yet discovered definitely, but I have to confess I have not been through the mass of Lee's papers now at the Shakespeare Centre in Stratford and not yet fully sorted. I will advance a theory in due course, for this rift.

Bullen won a scholarship to Worcester College, Oxford, in 1875, three years before Beeching and Lee went up to Balliol. Bullen took a first in Classical Mods. but like many distinguished men – A. E. Housman comes to mind — got only a third in Greats in 1879. That year he married Edith, a daughter of William John Goodwin, head of the map department of the Ecclesiastical Commissioners. In the different climate then, one cannot help wondering if some kind of emotional crisis had affected his class. The couple had two sons and three daughters, of whom I know little, but would like to learn if anyone can help me to trace them or their descendants.*

* The two sons died childless; of the daughters, Irene (Sidney Lee's god-daughter), was an unmarried school-teacher; Dorothea married Mr Henry and lived in Rouen; and Madge married an actor named Diffley and had a daughter Louise, born in 1917.

70

What exactly he did on coming down from Oxford is obscure; he seems to have been mixed up with the publishing world; he wrote some articles for the *DNB* under Sidney Lee. He immediately began editing a whole string of Elizabethan writers, though how these specialist texts could support a wife and growing family I cannot imagine. The first was John Day, which came out in 1881, followed by a collection of old plays which is still of use today, between 1882 and 1885. Then there was Paltock's *Peter Wilkins*, *Arden of Feversham*, Izaak Walton's *Lives*, Michael Drayton and so forth. He re-discovered Thomas Campion, published in 1889. This was a significant year for in the spring he gave six lectures in Oxford on Elizabethan writers, the basis of the posthumously published *Elizabethans*.

These lectures are rather interesting, for English was admitted as a subject for pass degrees at Oxford only in 1873 and the Honour School dates from 1896; the first Merton Professor was appointed in 1885. Who was behind the invitation to lecture I do not know, but Bullen seems to have had the knack of being acquainted with all the literary figures of his day, while his charming Irish manner is mentioned more than once. The late F. P. Wilson of Oxford called him "that breezy Elizabethan scholar"; he certainly knew the men, mostly slightly younger than himself, who edited and mapped out English literature of the sixteenth and seventeenth centuries in the early years of the twentieth century, such as Sir Walter Greg, to whom he suggested the editing of Henslowe's *Diary*; R. B. McKerrow, whom Bullen persuaded to edit Nashe; Oliver Elton was similarly asked to edit Drayton. He was also the friend of A. W. Pollard of the British Museum; Sir Edmund Chambers and Robert Bridges who both contributed to the "great" *Stratford Town Shakespeare*; E. Gordon Duff, the bibliographer; A. C. Swinburne; W. B. Yeats (of whom more in a moment); and George Gissing, whom Bullen paid £105 in advance for an unwritten novel in 1891 and eventually received *Denzil Quarnier*. He was, furthermore, one of the first to appreciate W. W. Jacobs.

But this is rather a digression from 1889; the Oxford lectures may have given him a taste for the academic life, and there is no doubt that if he had only been born 30 years later he could have settled down as an English teacher in some university or other and I would not have to tell you of his troubled later years. Anyhow, in 1889 the chair of English Language and Literature at University College, London, was vacant; Bullen applied but was unsuccessful – presumably that third in Greats pursued him. This was his last attempt to break into the academic world.

It is perhaps appropriate to say something here about Bullen from the scholarly angle. It has to be admitted that his editorial methods belonged to the old school and were nothing like as meticulous as those of his younger friends, Greg, McKerrow and Pollard. He did not have enough respect for his copy text, did not disdain intuitive readings or inspired guess-work. In his edition of Shakespeare he wrote "Conjectural emendations have been sparingly admitted, more sparingly than by Dyce, but the Cambridge Shakespeare has been judged to err on the side of ultra-conservatism". This is why his Shakespeare is of little scholarly value today. His importance in this field lies in his pioneer work in disinterring forgotten authors, his real knowledge and love of an immense range of Elizabethan and Jacobean writers and it was rather bad luck that he was ahead of his time in some ways but behind it in editorial standards. Some, though, have stood the test of time, such as the collection of old plays already mentioned, his *Lyrics from the song-books of the Elizabethan age*, and his posthumously published lectures entitled *Elizabethans* all of which have received attention from reprint publishers in recent years, a sure sign of worth. The text of his *Stratford Town Shakespeare* was used in a one volume edition of Shakespeare's *Works* published in 1934 by Basil Blackwell for the Shakespeare Head Press.

72

After failing to obtain an academic post, Bullen turned to publishing and in 1891 set up with Harold Lawrence, a man of literary and artistic interests and secretary of the Medici Society, as a partner at Henrietta Street, Covent Garden. H. F. B. Brett-Smith, in his *DNB* article on Bullen, aptly wrote that publishing was 'a career for which he had excellent literary intuition but small business capacity', and that really sums up the rest of his life – good ideas but no business ability to execute them. Lawrence & Bullen published mostly literature either of a rather avant-garde nature or of small popular appeal, such as Stanley's translation of Anacreon of 1651 which appeared in 1891 with a second impression in 1893. On p. xxiv Bullen wrote that it was done "purely from selfish motives – I wanted to read them once again with the advantage of fair type and ample margin" and that he had little leisure to complete the notes. It is a typical nice production of its period, but not outstanding. Percy Macquoid's finely produced *Dictionary of Furniture* and works by W. B. Yeats appeared under their imprint.

Katharine Tynan, in her autobiography *The wandering years* gives a pleasant picture of Bullen, who published some of her early works, as one who should have lived in the Elizabethan age; how he would wander about the English countryside drinking with ordinary folk in inns, a habit disliked by Lawrence. She adds "He was not to be found in London literary circles . . . Those were great days when Lawrence & Bullen published together and would have turned down the best sellers cheerfully . . . while holding out the hand to a poor poet or the young unknown just beginning. There was always tea when one called in the afternoons, and there was also whisky. Later on there was a partner, Hedley Peek. Lawrence used to say . . . 'Bullen, that whisky is going very fast', whereupon Bullen, shaking his head till the mane was all ruffled, would say 'Hedley can take his whack'." These business methods hardly made for financial success. The wandering habits are also revealed in letters to Gordon Duff, now in the Huntington Library in

California, from the 1890's, which mix up plans for books with those for fishing expeditions. Bullen was then living in Yelverton Villas in Twickenham, and mentions a happy Christmas with his children.

George Bullen died in 1894 and it is significant that the son published no more editions of Elizabethan writers after that date, though he did have plans for some right up to his death; perhaps the father supported the son financially till then.

The partnership with Lawrence lasted until 1900 and in that year he visited Ireland — the other factor in his heredity — where he seems to have had a drinking spree; one learns something of this trip from the correspondence of W. B. Yeats. In May, for instance, Yeats told Lady Gregory that he saw Bullen drunk in Dublin, while A. P. Watt, Yeats's literary agent, when told of this remarked "the better they are, the more they drink". Yeats unsuccessfully tried to persuade Bullen, in view of his Irish extraction, to settle in Dublin and publish Irish literature. But in 1901 Bullen found a new, young partner in Frank Sidgwick, then aged 22, who later founded the firm of Sidgwick & Jackson. Sidgwick, who came from a family of Oxford and Cambridge dons, claimed himself to have been the only member not to get a first at the university and so was set up in business, his father providing quite a large sum and his Rugby housemaster some more. Only Bullen's name, however, was put on imprints as Sidgwick was regarded more as an apprentice; he stayed with Bullen until March 1907. The Bodleian Library recently acquired the archives of the firm of Sidgwick & Jackson, which have not yet been fully sorted, but I have made a few forays among these papers. It is apparent that Sidgwick never got his money back and there is continuous correspondence over the years till Bullen's death with all kinds of schemes proposed — shares in projected publications, and so forth which rarely came to fruition. It must be emphasised that from this correspondence Sidgwick emerges as a most kind-hearted and likeable fellow and Bullen as a Micawber, eternally optimistic and full of hints how to deal with duns and bank managers; there is a fascinating description of how it is essential to keep a bank account moving, even if only a penny or so is involved, as from experience Bullen found that a static account only attracts the attention of a manager.

It is interesting that in Stratford Bullen is only remembered as a taciturn man who was always wandering about with an open book in his hand and a rough haired collie. This contrasts with the tales of his travels round the country drinking in small pubs, as Katharine Tynan and others recounted. Frank Sidgwick's Diary gives what must be regarded as the authoritative version of the story of Bullen's dream about visiting Stratford and being shown a copy of Shakespeare's works printed in his native town, and thinking that a good idea; the tale has frequently been repeated with variations. So far as the claim that the resulting *Stratford Town Shakespeare* was the first complete edition to be printed in the place of the author's birth is concerned, it should be pointed out here that actually an acting edition, suitable also for family reading, with the doubtful bits put in small type, had been printed by George Boyden, of the *Stratford Herald*, under the auspices of Charles Flower, between 1879 and 1891, but it was hardly a noble book and definitely not distinguished typographically. Its existence was rather underplayed on the frequent occasions Bullen's dream was repeated in print.

Bullen secured a house at 21 Chapel Street at a rent of £30 a year from the Corporation with effect from August 1904; it was next door but one to the site of New Place where Shakespeare had retired and where Julius Shaw, a witness to the poet's will, had lived — a fact that was duly publicised by Bullen. Frank Sidgwick established himself here and the Shakespeare Head Press was founded. Who chose the name is unknown; obviously, 'Shakespeare' was a necessary part, and 'Shakespeare Press' had been used both in Stratford and London by several firms. Later, about 1911,

William Jaggard, the compiler of a massive *Shakespeare Bibliography*, moved to Stratford from Liverpool and set up an antiquarian bookshop from which he published various works using the term 'Shakespeare Press', which annoyed Bullen and caused a certain amount of acrimonious correspondence, published and private, which lasted until Bullen's death.

21 Chapel Street was fitted up and a brochure printed which shows all the rooms in a remarkably tidy state before any work was done. An emblem, signed 'J A D' was devised from the First Folio portrait which has continued in use ever since; I wonder who the designer was.* Bullen here stated that "My aim is to print only good literature and to print it well." In June work began in earnest on volume one of the Shakespeare, styled the *Stratford Town Shakespeare*. Sidgwick spent most of his time in Stratford and Bullen mostly in London working from an office in Great Russell Street, and publishing continued from there. He was much involved in producing the early writings of W. B. Yeats; the latter found Bullen tended to ignore instructions, so the advice of Sydney Cockerell was sought and thereafter a firm line was adopted. Yeats wrote "Bullen always talks some kind of petulant nonsense before one gets a book out"; and on another occasion "I don't think he always listens very carefully to one's directions" and "It is a great mistake to humour him by giving in to him". It is apparent that Bullen did not hesitate to alter Yeats's text occasionally.

At Stratford there was first a Crown Broadside Mitre Press (valued at £95 in 1915), but it was found insufficient and in December 1905 a Double Crown Wharfedale by Payne was bought at a cost of £210; this did the bulk of the printing right up to Newdigate's time. At Stratford there was also a Demy Albion, valued at £23, signed "Jon. and Jer. Barret exors of R. W. Cope" which was one of the three once used by William Morris at the Kelmscott Press, and then by C. R. Ashbee at the Essex House Press. This machine came to Oxford with the rest of the firm in 1930

* *See p.* 88.

and was later loaned to the Printing Department of the Oxford School of Technology until 1972, and then given to the William Morris Society. It is now installed at Kelmscott House, Hammersmith. I am indebted to Sir Basil Blackwell for this information. A two horse power Crossley, Otto type K gas engine, valued at £65, provided the power.

Bullen's lack of business acumen has already been emphasised; W. B. Yeats wrote in 1902 "I have begun to have the greatest possible contempt for my dear Bullen's business capacity." This is very evident in the surviving ledgers and letter books now at the Shakespeare Centre in Stratford, which are scrappy and incomplete. It is painfully apparent that the whole affair was run on a shoe-string. Carbons for orders between 1905 and 1920 survive and the small amounts of paper from Spicer – two to five reams at a time; ink from Shackell Edwards, four pounds a time, and type quantities are very noticeable. Thus in March 1906, on different days, appear ½ lb of 14 pt Caslon Italic; 1½ lb Old Face Roman Ligatures; 6 lb of 8 pt quads. Orders went to Caslon's type foundry at almost weekly intervals. Caslon Old Face was used for the *Stratford Town Shakespeare*, in royal 8vo, with specially made paper by Spicer watermarked with the arms of Shakespeare. This does not seem very adventurous today, but Caslon Old Face was very much the fashionable fount at the time, as one can gather from Nicolas Barker's recent biography of Stanley Morison. Bullen was responsible for the text with a staff of four compositors and one press-man, while the binding was done by a London firm (? James Burn) and the plates by Emery Walker were also printed there.

The first volume came out in November 1904, three in 1905, five in 1906 and the last in January 1907. Each was between 300 and 400 pages. It can be described as pleasant, but not distinguished. Twelve copies were printed on vellum. No expense was spared and various distinguished people contributed essays, mostly friends like H. C. Beeching and J. J. Jusserand, or Robert Bridges whose paper on the influence of the audience on Shakespeare was reprinted in New York in 1926 by Doubleday & Page, one of Stanley Morison's first productions in Monotype. Yeats and Swinburne declined invitations to contribute. Another significant absentee was his old schoolfellow Sidney Lee, whose *Life of Shakespeare*, regarded as a standard work for many years, had first been published in 1898. I do not know what happened, but Bullen did not move his family to Stratford. Instead he lived with two ladies, Edith and Alys Lister, called his cousins, but the relationship is obscure. From Edith Lister's correspondence with Frank Sidgwick, 1920–38, it would appear that Sidney Lee took Mrs Bullen's side in whatever the quarrel was, and I must say that she must have had a harrowing time if she had to look after a husband and five children with Bullen's precarious finances. But no expense was spared and a thousand copies, priced at ten guineas besides the twelve on vellum were printed.* There were about 500 sets left in 1915, when an inventory was made, but it is evident that varying numbers of each volume were printed.

Bullen had, typically, been unduly optimistic and does not seem to have made very efficient estimates of costs, prices or sales, and he got heavily into debt. The result was that Frank Sidgwick left, on friendly terms, in March 1907 to set up on his own with Jackson and with Bullen's stock of London publications. There was no money to repay what Sidgwick's father and housemaster had put up, so Sidgwick became the owner of the Press, Bullen paying him a rent of £8.8.6 a month, and was given a set of the *Stratford Town Shakespeare* on vellum, which Bullen valued at a thousand pounds till one came up at Sotheby's in 1910 and made only £33.

In what I take to have been an emergency measure, Bullen took on in 1906, at the invitation of Lord Northcliffe, the editorship of the *Gentleman's Magazine*, then on its last legs, and it only ran to eleven more numbers, ceasing in September 1907; typical, I fear, of the failure that was

* *FS diary shows six sold.*

78

pursuing Bullen. From the almost daily letters to Sidgwick at this time, it is evident that Bullen had no money at all, and could not pay the wages of his men nor the rent of the house. He seems to have survived by getting loans from, among others, Lord Plymouth and Mrs Davies, the mother of the two ladies who later founded the Gregynog Press; he also had hopes of Northcliffe giving a lot of cash, but in spite of many half-promises none ever came. Without any documentary evidence, I venture to think that these loans were used to pay Sidgwick.

Bullen now gave up his London office completely and settled in Stratford with the Misses Lister; Edith was a writer who published verse under the pseudonym of E. M. Martin and magazine stories and articles under a variety of names. Alys seems to have been the Martha of the pair. Edith acted as secretary of the Press and was the fierce champion of Bullen for the rest of her life; she died in 1938 when F. C. Wellstood, then Director of Shakespeare's Birthplace, had the foresight to remove all the papers he could find in the house, without which I could not be telling this tale.

Yeats, who visited Stratford in December 1907, bore witness to Bullen's financial distress. He was being pressed for payment by James Burn & Co., the London binders, whose records were unfortunately destroyed in the 1939–45 War.

But to get back to actual books; besides the *Stratford Town Shakespeare*, Bullen was also printing various small volumes, such as *Venus and Adonis* in December 1905; the printers' flowers border on the title was a distinct innovation and an imitation of a late sixteenth- early seventeenth-century style. The spelling was modernised and is typical of the house style used by Bullen and quite good of its period but not outstanding; it is definitely superior to *Innocencies* by Katharine Tynan, the Irish poetess, also 1905, with the London imprint but printed in Stratford, as can be seen from the colophon. The Anacreon of 1906 in Stanley's translation is similar; it is an amended reprint of Bullen's edition of 1892–3 and incidentally reveals that there was no Greek type available; the Preface was also rewritten to avoid having to use the odd Greek word found in the earlier version. It also presumably helped to work off surplus stock of J. R. Weguelin's rather luscious plates. A more interesting style is found in the six Shakespeare Head Booklets, which sold fairly well, probably to tourists; again the arabesque title-page border is used. Katharine Adams, then starting her career as a binder in nearby Broadway, sometimes bound all six in one volume, which are now collectors' pieces.

Like all private or semi-private presses (and here I think the Shakespeare Head, so far as Bullen was concerned, was intended really as a commercial enterprise, even if so precarious) a certain number of volumes of poor verse were produced, usually paid for by the authors themselves; a typical example was *Chosen Poems* by W. J. Ibett of 1915. After Bullen's death, this author sent a demand for royalties, which both worried and amused Edith Lister who consulted Frank Sidgwick and revealed that actually money had been lost on the project.

After Bullen left London for good, he showed the same interest in the books published in Stratford. The sixteenth and seventeenth-centuries in English literature were represented for example, by editions of William Drummond of Hawthornden's *Conversations with Ben Jonson*, and by Drayton's *Nimphidia* of 1908. Irish literature in plays by Charles McEvoy, a minor member of the Yeats–Lady Gregory circle; and by Stephen McKenna's translation of Plotinus, *On the beautiful*, which had some success as it was reprinted three times after its first appearance in 1908. Bullen also printed numerous plays by Yeats in cheap editions.

In 1908 Bullen embarked on a complete edition of Yeats's *Works*; possibly this was intended as a kindness on the author's part, as he was then only 43; 1,060 copies were printed of the eight volumes of which Chapman & Hall took 250. Bullen treated the living Yeats as if he were a dead Elizabethan writer and arbitrarily emended the text without

80

consultation, annoying Yeats and causing him to have a proper agreement drawn up by his agent, A. P. Watt. Obviously, there was little work on hand for the Press; all eight volumes were produced in the second half of 1908; Yeats estimated that each volume of 250 to 300 pages would take seven or eight weeks to set up and print, but Bullen was only taking three. Although two-thirds of the copies sold, this was another financial disaster, in spite of financial help of £3,455 from Miss A. E. F. Horniman, which, incidentally, Bullen did not hesitate to divert into other channels as his letters to Sidgwick reveal. In 1919 Yeats was still owed £30, so he settled for two sets of the *Stratford Town Shakespeare* and one set of the six-volume *Works* of Mrs. Aphra Behn. Arthur Waugh, of Chapman & Hall, was of the same opinion as everyone else about Bullen's business capabilities, writing that he was "first and foremost a man; then a man of letters, and last of all a publisher".

The bad financial position after finishing Yeats' *Works* is reflected in the few productions of the Press during the next two years, and it can only be assumed that he had to get rid of his printing staff. In 1909, only two small pamphlets appeared: Yeats's *Cathleen ni Houlihan* and *Advance sheets from the Globe and Blackfriars* by that difficult scholar, C. W. Wallace, presumably paid for by him. Note that the imprint on *Cathleen* merely says "London: A. H. Bullen"; he was using W. W. Gibbings as agents. In 1910 only Yeats's *Poems: Second Series*, of 164 pages appeared. I should say that several leaflets listing past publications were also printed.

In 1910 Bullen first mooted the idea that the Shakespeare Head Press should be endowed as a permanent memorial to Shakespeare in order to print scholarly works of little commercial value. He wanted £12,000. He persuaded Lord Northcliffe to publicise the appeal in the *Daily Mail* in 1910 and 1911, and he did obtain some support, but not a great deal. Mrs Davies of Llandinam, responded, as also did a few Stratford people, such as George Boyden, the benevolent proprietor of the local newspaper. Bullen took the attitude that it was the duty of the country to support this project and this was also energetically put forward by Edith Lister – a point of view I find rather distasteful. About £800 was subscribed in all. Bullen also secured a small Civil List pension in 1912 through the influence of the Prime Minister, Asquith, who had been at school with him, and Percy Withers.

The charitable donations enabled the Press to revive a little. Seven plays by Yeats were printed in 1911. Bullen was full of plans, as can be seen from a leaflet put out in 1912. His criterion that a book must have real use and interest rather than profitability, though admirable in theory, helps to explain his tribulations.

During the next few years, all sorts of books began to be produced by the Press, including some of Edith Lister's writings under the name of E. M. Martin; and others by Leslie B. Taylor, of the Westley Richards firm of gunmakers, who wrote verse under the pseudonym of Lawrence Forth; editions of Shakespeare's *Poems* and one or two scholarly works, such as the two series of W. J. Lawrence's *Elizabethan Playhouse*, a pioneer study; Lacy Collison-Morley's *Shakespeare in Italy*; Gabriel Harvey's *Marginalia*, edited by G. C. Moore Smith; and Mrs Aphra Behn's *Works* in six volumes edited (and partly paid for) by Montague Summers shared with Heinemann. The house style remained the same.*

The tercentenary of Shakespeare's death in 1916 not surprisingly prompted Bullen to revive his appeal for an endowment, but again did he not meet with much success; £382 was contributed. Sir Edward Brabrook acted as

---

* Mr Ralph Edwards, the authority on furniture history, whose father was Rector of Tredington, not far from Stratford, has told me something of the Press when he helped Bullen for a short time during the early years of the 1914–18 War. His chief recollections are the lack of work and a great amount of talk about future publications that never came out; there was then only one journeyman employed by the Press.

honorary treasurer, and on his death in 1932 Edith Lister was astonished to learn from his executors that a balance of £240 remained, which was handed over to the Shakespeare Association on her suggestion. The War was also beginning to have an effect and output declined again. Bullen wrote several patriotic poems against the Germans which he printed as broadsides. In 1915 James Burn & Co., the binders, after what I must say was exemplary patience over delays in settling accounts, took a quantity of stock as payment; while most of Yeats's writings were handed over to Macmillan to pay for £143 outstanding as royalties. A valuation of equipment and stock was made in December 1915 and how the crisis was resolved, I do not know; perhaps more kind friends helped, for the Press continued its small output. Twelve volumes of Visitors' Books for 1905–20 have survived among the Lister papers; there was obviously a continuous stream, but it would appear that not many sales were made.

The last complete book that Bullen saw published at the Press was a little volume of *Shakespeare's Songs*, one of several editions produced for the tourist trade, and still in the same typographical style of the early books. A new edition of Shakespeare's *Sonnets* was well advanced, with the text printed but awaiting the editor's notes, as H. F. B. Brett-Smith described in his Foreword when published in 1921, a year after Bullen's death on 29 February 1920, aged only 63. He was worn out, it is said, by worry over his Press, the War and actual want. His estate consisted of £1.10 cash; sale of his clothes £10; his private library, though, was valued at £287. His brother Edward, a Plymouth solicitor, helped to clear up. None of his family appeared, but his widow received £3.10 – presumably outstanding maintenance; she was not mentioned in his will. Edith Lister was given his manuscripts. He was buried at Luddington, where a plain oak plank marks his grave, inscribed with his name, dates and "Scholar and gentleman".

Edith Lister dealt with the main assets of the Press, its

equipment and stock, but she insisted that it must stay in Stratford as a memorial to Shakespeare and Bullen; she valued it at £2,660. First an Indian Maharajah showed an interest, as a place to train Indian printers. Thomas Jones, secretary to the Cabinet and friend of Lloyd George and the Davies family of Llandinam, tried to secure the equipment to transfer to Wales to start the Gregynog Press for the Misses Davies; there were other nibbles from such as Dr. Rosenberg of New York. Then Basil Blackwell began negotiations, formed a company and acquired the Press for £1,500 plus £492 for stock. This was used to pay Miss A. E. F. Horniman, Montagu Summers (£75), Lord Plymouth (£25) and the Misses Lister (£310) about a third of what had been advanced. Unknown to the new owners, Edith Lister had set up and printed about 200 copies of a small collection of poems by Bullen, but she never distributed them; apart from one given to Frank Sidgwick and now in the Sidgwick & Jackson archives, all are still in sheets among her papers at Stratford.

B. H. Newdigate was appointed to oversee the Press, with a young Oxford graduate, Wilfrid Blair-Fish, from a Midland family, with literary interests, as manager. The latter had had a verse play printed at the Press in 1916; he died a year or two ago at Fladbury. That, however, is another and happier tale; there was a typographical revolution and the books for which the Shakespeare Head Press is famous began to appear. The first one was a little *Nimphidia* by Drayton; compare it with Bullen's edition of 1908 and the contrast both in style and scholarly methods is immediately apparent; the 1921 one follows the 1627 edition in spelling and the few changes are noted in the Preface; Bullen's text had been modernised with no explanations. Frankly, Bullen's books had been rather ordinary; now the Press became distinguished. During his regime, 150 items had been produced, including ephemera and jobbing work, of which 67 per cent had been literary, including 21 per cent of Irish items and 25 per cent Elizabethan or Jacobean; another 9

84

per cent was literary criticism; another 35 per cent had been lists of publications, appeals, letter heads, bills and so forth. Under Newdigate, the literary output rose to 77 per cent, with no Irish items, and the jobbing fell to 10 per cent. But Bullen certainly showed a more pioneering spirit in his rescuing of forgotten authors, his work for Irish writers and his encouragement of scholarly studies.

Two works by Bullen were published posthumously: his lectures, *Elizabethans* (recently reprinted) and *Weeping-Cross and other Rimes*, published by Sidgwick & Jackson with the only known photograph. Both had forewords by Edith Lister under different initials. This rather depressing story can be ended with Bullen's poem *Weeping-Cross* which summarises his career:

> *With bold heart, high-aspiring aim*
> *Forth fared he in the morning gray,*
> *To storm the Citadel of Fame*
> *And win a crown of fadeless bay:*
> *Ungarlanded, at day's decline,*
> *Ruefully weighing gain with loss,*
> *When neither moon nor star did shine,*
> *Homeward he stole by Weeping-Cross.*

11th November 1917

85

HERE ENDS THE *STRATFORD TOWN* EDITION
OF THE WORKS OF WILLIAM SHAKESPEARE
IN TEN VOLUMES PRINTED FOR A. H. BULLEN
& F. SIDGWICK AT THE *SHAKESPEARE HEAD*
PRESS, STRATFORD-ON-AVON, IN THE HOUSE
OF JULIUS SHAW THE POET'S FRIEND & ONE
OF THE WITNESSES TO HIS WILL. THE TEXT
REVISED BY A. H. BULLEN. WITH ESSAYS BY
H. C. BEECHING, ROBERT BRIDGES, HENRY
DAVEY, E. K. CHAMBERS, J. J. JUSSERAND &
M. H. SPIELMANN

TYPE COMPOSED UNDER THE SUPERVISION
OF T. E. SUMMERTON BY J. H. PICKWORTH,
W. H. WESSON & E. EBORALL, NATIVES OF
STRATFORD-ON-AVON; THE WHOLE PRINTED
BY F. S. COOPER. THE PROOFS THROUGHOUT
READ BY C. T. WHITE & THE EDITOR; IN PART
BY F. SIDGWICK, A. F. WALLIS, & C. G. TENNANT.
THE WORK BEGUN IN JULY, M.CM.IV
AND FINISHED IN JANUARY
M.CM.VII

APPENDIX B: LETTER FROM FRANK SIDGWICK TO BERNARD NEWDIGATE

9 Nov. 1927

Dear Newdigate,

I have had to do a bit of research to answer your question, but I was piqued to find I had forgotten the designer's name, so please don't feel any compunction at having "troubled" me.

I kept a careful diary of the first ten months of the Press, and find that the blocks of the S.H.P. device arrived on 19 Sept. 1904. But I had no note of the designer's name, as the design was commissioned by Bullen in London. However, I remembered that he had consulted Jacobi about it, so I wrote on receipt of your letter to Jacobi, who remembered the engraver but not the designer, and sent me on to the Chiswick Press, where an old address-book furnished the facts.

The designer was, as Jacobi recalled, a "young Scotsman", and the C.P. address-book showed his name as J. A. Duncan (which I thereupon remembered), with an address, thought to be out of date, at Boquhan, Balfron, N.B. Jacobi has an impression, however, that he is dead.

The engraver of the wood-block (which I suppose is in your hands) was an old friend of Jacobi's, Percy Roberts, who he says died in 1916 aged 83. He was an old apprentice of Landell's, the famous engraver, contemporary of W. J. Linton.

To the best of my recollection, the woodblock was three inches high (major axis), and we started with two electros of the same size, and three of half-size ($1\frac{1}{2}$ ins).

And when all's said and done, it is not a very beautiful device!

Yours sincerely,
F.S.

APPENDIX C: THE SIDGWICKS

FRANK SIDGWICK, who wrote this diary, was the son of Arthur Sidgwick. He was a Classics master at Rugby at the time of Frank's birth in 1879. Shortly after this the family moved to Oxford where Arthur became a don at Corpus Christi, a position he held for the rest of his working life.

There he delighted generations of undergraduates with his enthusiasm for Greek poetry, his beautiful reading and his witty conversation.

A caricature of him, drawn by Max Beerbohm when an undergraduate, shows him skipping over Mount Parnassus with his beard and gown flowing out behind him. He published several Latin and Greek primers which were used in preparatory schools for generations, and by their light-hearted composition must have eased the learning of those languages for thousands of unwilling little boys.

His brother Henry was professor of Moral Philosophy at Cambridge and the author of several books on ethics and philosophy, the most important being *The Methods of Ethics*. With his wife Eleanor he founded Newnham College, Cambridge.

Their only sister, Minnie, married a cousin, Edward Benson (later Archbishop of Canterbury) and become the mother of the writers E. F. Benson and A. C. Benson.

Frank, who was Arthur's third child and elder son, was educated, like all Oxford dons' sons, at the then new school later known as the Dragon School, whose headmaster, C. C. Lynam, became his life-long friend. He then went to Rugby and to Trinity College, Cambridge.

On leaving Cambridge he joined the book publishing firm of A. H. Bullen, where he stayed (with the months in Stratford in 1904/5) until 1907. During this time he published, in collaboration with E. K. Chambers, *Early English Lyrics* and some selections of ballads, a subject on which he became an authority.

In 1908 he founded his own publishing firm, Sidgwick and Jackson Ltd. Jackson was killed in 1917 and his co-director from then on was Dr R. B. McKerrow, a well known bibliographer and expert on early printed books. It was McKerrow who held the firm together in the latter part of the 1914/18 war when Frank was in the army. Frank published two books of light verse, *Some Verse* and *More Verse*, further collections of ballads, and in the 1930s with Robert Swann *The Making of Verse*. He married Mary Coxhead, daughter of A. C. Coxhead who was also a friend of A. H. Bullen and of Hedley Peek (see page 73). Frank died suddenly just after his 60th birthday in August 1939.

Of Arthur's other children, the eldest, Rose, was professor of history at Birmingham University until her early death in 1919 in the flu epidemic. Ethel became the author of a number of novels; Margie must still be remembered by many in north Oxford where she lived till she died in the 1940s, and Hugh, the most brilliant, the author of *Walking Essays*, *The Promenade Ticket* and *Jones's Wedding*, was killed in Flanders in 1917.

The similarities that ran all through this family seem to be a delight in literature, especially poetry: an ability to write verse, especially parodies: a passion for education, especially female: an inclination towards liberal politics: a love of walking in the English countryside: and an irrepressible verbal wit which they would sprinkle into any conversation, to the consternation of those plodders who could only consider serious matters in serious terms.

ANN BAER

THE Shakespeare Head Press has
been established to do honour to
Shakespeare's memory by printing and
publishing in Stratford-on-Avon a worthy
edition of his Works. Some years ago an
"acting" edition of the plays was issued
from a Stratford press; but hitherto no
complete edition of Shakespeare's Works,
carefully edited and handsomely printed,
has been published in his native town.

This standing reproach is removed by
the "Stratford Town Shakespeare." At
the Shakespeare Head Press will be composed, printed, and published a collected
edition (in ten volumes) that will take rank
with the finest *éditions de luxe* issued from
London, Oxford, and Edinburgh.

IN 1597 Shakespeare purchased New Place; and in the same year Julius Shaw, wool-striker and maltster, obtained from the Stratford Corporation a twenty-five years' lease of the house standing two doors to the north of New Place. Shaw was an intimate friend of Shakespeare and one of the witnesses to his will. The Stratford Corporation, which is still the owner of the property, has granted to the SHAKESPEARE HEAD PRESS a lease of the house that Julius Shaw occupied. Though the frontage and parts of the interior have been renewed, the main structure of the building is unchanged. From this old Tudor house, where Shakespeare must have been a frequent guest, the "Stratford Town" edition of his collected works will be issued.

THE "Stratford Town Shakespeare" consists of ten super-royal octavo volumes (seven by ten-and-an-eighth inches), printed in the original Old Face type cut by William Caslon in the early part of the eighteenth century. For the text is used the size known as "English," the songs, etc., being printed in small pica. The lines are numbered at the side. To each volume is prefixed a frontispiece.

The volumes will be tastefully bound in buckram.

An English hand-made paper, with Shakespeare's crest and coat-of-arms for watermark, has been specially manufactured for this edition.

A Prospectus, with specimen page, will be sent on application.

THE TEXT

THE text has been prepared for press by Mr. A. H. Bullen. Conjectural emendations have been sparingly admitted, more sparingly than by Dyce, but the " Cambridge Shakespeare " has been judged to err on the side of ultra-conservatism.

TERMS OF SUBSCRIPTION.

THE " Stratford Town Shakespeare " will be published in Ten Volumes at One Guinea *net* per volume, sold only in sets. A reduction of ten per cent. is made to subscribers who pay in advance for their sets.

The edition is strictly limited to One Thousand numbered copies.

Please enter my name as a subscriber for   cop   of " The Stratford Town Shakespeare " in Ten Volumes, at One Guinea per volume.

(*a*) I agree to pay for each volume upon delivery.

(*b*) I enclose nine guineas in prepayment for the ten volumes.

Name:—

Address:—

Date:—

VELLUM COPIES.

TWELVE copies have been printed on pure vellum.   Price will be sent on application.

EXTRA-BOUND COPIES.

COPIES will be supplied in quires for extra binding; or can be had in special leather binding from the SHAKESPEARE HEAD PRESS.

VIEW FROM GARDEN.

ONE of the most curious and striking objects in the SHAKESPEARE HEAD PRESS is the broad, massive chimney. The main shaft runs right through the house, and at the base, into which the Tudor Mantelpiece (p. 7) is fitted, it is more than six feet in thickness. The ornamentation of the part above the roof is unique in Stratford, but the chimneys of the alms-houses, adjacent to the Grammar School, are somewhat similar in design.

TUDOR MANTELPIECE
(on the ground floor).

THE fine Tudor mantelpiece, in the front room on the ground floor, has happily been preserved in its original state uninjured and undisturbed. It dates back beyond Shakespeare's time to the days of Henry VII.

THE OAK-PANELLED ROOM.

THE antique oak-panelling has been overlaid with paint, but is being carefully restored to its original condition. The moulding is identical with that of the recessed-cupboard doors, and is bolted with wood staples in the ancient manner.

This room is used as the printing and publishing office of the SHAKESPEARE HEAD PRESS.

COMPOSING ROOM.

THE ancient Kitchen—perhaps the least altered room of any in the house —has been converted into a composing room.

The machine-room, forming the end-gable of the back part of the house (see the photograph on p. 6), is of the same age, and is traditionally known as " the brew-house."

A STORE ROOM.

THIS old room is used for the storing of paper, printed and unprinted. On the glass panes of the leaded window have been scratched the names of former occupiers. It is a low-roofed room, situated immediately over the old kitchen now used as a composing-room.

THE GARDEN.

THE garden "circummured with brick" had been allowed to fall into neglect, but is now being converted into an old-time pleasaunce—"with fairest flowers whilst summer lasts" and "the pleached bower." A time-worn wall of rich red brick separates it from New Place Gardens.

SIXTEENTH CENTURY ATTICS.

FROM the windows of the upper pair of attics is a good view over New Place Gardens.

SIXTEENTH CENTURY ATTICS.

THESE untouched attics are used as "drying-rooms" for the printed sheets of vellum and paper.

THE MODERNISED FRONTAGE.

THE front of the old house has been modernised, though at no recent date, as may be gathered from the "blind" window on the first floor, significant of the days of "window-tax."

Visitors to Stratford-on-Avon are cordially invited to call at THE SHAKESPEARE HEAD PRESS *and inspect the "Stratford Town Edition."*